Praise for *A Cross-Sh*

Bryan Loritts reminds us that Jesus Christ didn̶ take over. He didn't come to just redeem us, b *Gospel* is a thoughtful book that will challenge your creed and conduct.

—Dr. Dennis Rainey
host, FamilyLife Today

I have had the privilege of doing life and leadership with Bryan Loritts for the past eight years. I can promise you that the words on these pages of *A Cross-Shaped Gospel* are not merely wishful thoughts or untested ideals. They are the learned lessons of daily blood, sweat, and tears coupled with occasional smiles and celebrations. As Bryan has led us toward a cross-shaped church, we have been blessed to have front row seats to watch evidences of God's grace as we have labored to bring God glory, show off Jesus, and live out the gospel in Memphis and beyond . . . vertically and horizontally!

—Dr. John W. Bryson
Fellowship Memphis

Bryan is a great thinker and wise leader, and has become a leader of leaders. I always come away encouraged and thinking in new categories after hearing what he has to say. Above all he loves Christ and God's people. I'd encourage you to listen to Him if you want to love Christ more and lead His people well.

—Dr. Rick McKinley
lead pastor of Imago Dei Community and
author of *A Kingdom Called Desire*

Bryan is my son. He has ministered to me in deep profound ways . . . I say this not because I am a proud father (I am!), but because of Bryan's love and passion for the gospel and his faithfulness to the Word of God. Bryan's heart and passion is given to us in *A Cross-Shaped Gospel*. As you read this book, your heart and mind will be moved in fresh ways by the power of the cross!

—Dr. Crawford W. Loritts Jr.
author, speaker, radio host
senior pastor, Fellowship Bible Church
Roswell, Georgia

In the four years I have come to know Bryan Loritts, he has helped me think more deeply, love more widely, submit to the gospel more humbly, live more passionately, share Jesus more freely, and engage the world more missionally. One of the church's rising young leaders, Bryan is the real deal, more interested in living for a cause than building a pedestal. We need more Christian leaders like him.

I am convinced that when you read *A Cross-Shaped Gospel*, you will be peeking into the heart of a man whose love for God radiates to the thousands who hear him speak and to those who call him friend. This is a rare combination.

—Barry Corey
president of Biola University

Bryan Loritts passionately lives what he writes about in *A Cross-Shaped Gospel*. Moving to Memphis, Bryan determined to dynamically work out both the theology and praxis of loving God and loving our neighbor in a context of real world, civil rights tensions.

—Dave Gibbons
author of *XEALOTS: Defying the
Gravity of Normality*

Bryan Loritts is an unusually anointed pastor/exegete/preacher/present-day prophet sent by God for such a time as this. He has a unique gift of spiritual discernment that comes forth with practical and powerful applications that God uses to confront, challenge, and change lives. His communication style is driven by a passion for biblical truth, a discipline of exegetical investigation, and a love for his Lord that is more often reserved and displayed in men of God with far more time on this spiritual journey called life. Prepare to be blessed by the refreshing revelation of eternal truths that God releases through Bryan Loritts.

—Dr. Kenneth C. Ulmer
president, The King's University
senior pastor, Faithful Central Bible Church
Los Angeles, CA

Bryan has provided us with a rare jewel helpful for every believer to understand the centrality of the gospel in our everyday lives. Bryan's work is a invaluable for every believer to gain a fresh appreciation for reclaiming the gospel for our everyday lives. We too often allow our own biases to distort the power of the cross but this work reminds us that only through the cross can we gain the power to love God and others. Bryan is an amazingly fresh and clear voice that the world desperately needs to hear. His writings are biblical, relevant, engaging, and insightful. Bryan's life work is to be a transformational bridge builder, and this work is a testament to his ability to bring the church together to remember what's most important—the cross and the gospel. A long overdue work to challenge all of us to live out the true meaning of the cross both horizontally and vertically

—Bryan L. Carter
senior pastor, Concord Church
Dallas, TX

a CROSS-SHAPED Gospel

Gospel

Reconciling Heaven and Earth

BRYAN LORITTS

MOODY PUBLISHERS

CHICAGO

All Scripture quotations, unless otherwise indicated, are taken from *The Holy Bible, English Standard Version*, copyright © 2000, 2001 by Crossway Bibles, a division of Good News Publishers. Used by permission. All rights reserved.

Scripture quotations marked AMP are taken from *The Amplified Bible*, copyright © 1965, 1987 by The Zondervan Corporation. *The Amplified New Testament* copyright © 1958, 1987 by The Lockman Foundation. Used by permission.

Edited by Jim Vincent
Interior design: Ragont Design
Cover design: Thinkpen Design

Library of Congress Cataloging-in-Publication Data

Loritts, Bryan C.
  A cross-shaped Gospel : reconciling Heaven and earth / Bryan Loritts.
     p. cm.
  Includes bibliographical references.
  ISBN 978-0-8024-0065-9
  1. Christian sociology. 2. Love—Religious aspects—Christianity. I. Title.
  BT738.L615 2011
  241'.4—dc23

                                                2011023244

Moody Publishers
820 N. LaSalle Boulevard
Chicago, IL 60610

1 3 5 7 9 10 8 6 4 2

Printed in the United States of America

To Ricky Jenkins and Albert Tate,
my sons in the ministry, and on the cusp of greatness.
May your ministry be marked by
living and preaching the cross-shaped gospel.

CONTENTS

INTRODUCTION: FROM THE SHADOW OF THE CROSS

In Holman Hunt's classic painting, Jesus comes to the end of what appears to be another long workday at His father's carpentry shop. He is stripped to the waist and stretching, and the light of dusk seeps through the room at such an angle that a shadow appears in the form of a cross on the wall behind Jesus. Even the most unaware observer can't miss the artist's point: In His youth, Jesus could never escape the cross—it hovered over Him daily.[1]

No other symbol in the history of humanity has become as iconic as the cross. Instantly recognized by millions of people, the cross has inspired hope and courage, and brought new life to untold numbers of people since the scandalous, but necessary, death of Jesus Christ. To Holman Hunt, the cross, "the emblem of suffering and shame,"[2] was not just a historical event, or even symbolic of a future hope, but a living reality.

When Jesus instructed His followers to take up their cross and follow Him (Matthew 16:24), He envisioned a whole new way of living. In one of many paradoxical statements, Jesus said that true life could come only through death, the death of the cross. To His disciples Jesus said, "And whoever does not take his cross and follow me is not worthy of me. Whoever finds his life will lose it, and whoever loses his life for my sake will find it" (Matthew 10:38–39). Jesus drew a parallel between the cross and life—a life that doesn't just begin when I'm buried, but a life that begins in the present, the moment I give my life to Jesus and cling to the "old rugged cross."

> The two beams of the cross—one vertical, the other horizontal—tell us all we need to know about the gospel.

The gospel and the cross are intertwined, so closely related that you cannot see one without the other. The gospel *is* the cross. In fact, we need not look far to get a very clear picture of the gospel; just look at its shape. The two beams of the cross—one vertical, the other horizontal—tell us all we need to know about the gospel. The cross-shaped gospel has to do with man being reconciled to God (the vertical beam) and to one another (the horizontal beam) through the sacrifice of Jesus Christ, the Messiah who died in our place and for our sins. Sadly, many times we disconnect the two beams, undermining the power of the gospel. When we disconnect the vertical and horizontal beams, the Christ-follower and the church limp along, not functioning at full capacity.

Oh, but the beauty of the cross-shaped gospel is when both dimensions are lived out through a life that has been justified and growing in Christ-exalting holiness, along with loving and engaging our neighbors and society for the glory of God. Church and life just doesn't get any better than when we are living the cross-shaped gospel.

Life is at its richest when we are living in close communion with God and loving our neighbors at the same time. When life becomes solely about quiet times and Bible studies, there's this innate feeling that something is missing, because something is! On the other hand, when life is just about serving and loving others, and it doesn't flow from deep affections for God, a sense of disequilibrium creeps in as well.

The cross-shaped gospel isn't ultimately about *our* enjoyment or living *my* life to the fullest. These are but by-products of two greater realities—the glory of God and the betterment of our world. My prayer for you, as you begin this book, is that God will be even more glorified in your life, and that your spheres of influence are bettered because you're living this cross-shaped gospel.

1 THE GOSPEL IN TWO-PART HARMONY

At every forward step and movement, at every
going in and out . . . in all the ordinary actions of
daily life, we trace upon the forehead the cross.[1]

Tertullian

Albert Einstein was boarding a train one day, clearly preoccupied
with something. While the other passengers were settling into their seats
and preparing for the journey ahead, Dr. Einstein was frantically scanning
the floors, lost in a search. One of the train crew noticed this and asked the
brilliant scientist what he was trying to find. Albert responded that he
had lost his ticket. The conductor waved the renowned Einstein off, assur-
ing him that he need not look for his ticket because he knew exactly who
he was. This was the man, after all, whom *Time* magazine would eventually label "the man of the twentieth century." His discoveries in physics
would astound the world and change how we view the universe.

But still, Dr. Albert Einstein continued his quest for the ticket, looking between the seats and down the aisles, ignoring the conductor. Some
moments later this same man reiterated that Albert didn't need to worry
about finding his ticket, because again, everyone knew who he was, and
surely this world-famous professor and Nobel laureate would not try to
scam his way onto a train. "Relax, Dr. Einstein, we all know who you are,"
the conductor said.

With a frustrated sigh, Professor Einstein responded, "It's not that I don't know who I am, I know exactly who I am. I'm looking for my ticket because I don't know where I'm going."[2]

The "Who Am I" and "Where Am I Going" Questions

Einstein's response to the train worker unearths for us two fundamental questions that every human being must face: (1) Who am I? and (2) Where am I going? Identity and direction lie at the core of humanity's soul. Fail to find the answers to these core questions, and life will be devoid of any possible meaning or satisfaction. Humanity's problem is not that men and women aren't looking for the answers to these questions; it's that most of them will spend their lives filling the blank spaces of their souls with the wrong answers.

So where can the right answers be found? Saul of Tarsus, a devout Jew, realized later in life he had been pursuing the answers for identity and direction in the wrong places. A well-educated man and very religious, he had been proud of his status as being from the same tribe of Israel that birthed her first king. As a religious Pharisee, he no doubt thought his identity could be found in his pedigree, education, and religion. He says so in Philippians 3:4–6. Yet later on Saul realized Jesus was the Christ, and he would become the humble apostle Paul. That brought about a remarkable change in attitude. His identity was no longer in himself. He wrote, "But whatever gain I had, I counted as loss for the sake of Christ. Indeed, I count everything as loss because of the surpassing worth of knowing Christ Jesus my Lord. For his sake I have suffered the loss of all things and count them as rubbish, in order that I may gain Christ" (Philippians 3:7–8).

Paul admits that he had spent his life pursuing the wrong answer, yet on a dusty Damascus road one day all of that changed when his life was transformed and revolutionized by the gospel of Jesus Christ. Now in Christ he had found identity. That's why he told the Corinthians that if we are in Christ, we are a new creation (see 2 Corinthians 5:17).

The gospel of Jesus Christ answers all of the questions and longings of our soul. Who am I? I am a child of God in relationship with the creator of the universe (John 1:12) because of the gospel. Where am I going? My direction and aim in life is found in the gospel.

Moving toward the *Zoe* Life

Since the gospel addresses our most basic needs and essential questions, God is most honored and life becomes alive when we have as our sole operating system the gospel of Jesus Christ—or what we will call in this book, the cross-shaped gospel. This is what Jesus taught His disciples when He announced that He had come "that they may have life and have it abundantly" (John 10:10).

The Greeks had two primary words for *life*: *bios* (we get such words as *biology* from here) and *zoe*. *Bios* has to do with pure existence; you know, inhaling and exhaling. *Zoe*, on the other hand, refers to life on a qualitative level. *Zoe* describes a life rich with meaning, value, and significance. One of the great tragedies of life is that most people have *bios* life but not *zoe* life. According to Jesus, *zoe* living is found in Him and therefore in the gospel.

Most of us will live longer than the disciples did here on earth. By today's standards, these men died relatively young. Very few of us, however, will have truly *lived* like they did, having that *zoe* life of value and significance. These men whom Jesus handpicked were so consumed by the gospel that they changed cities and their world. Along the way, they established churches that didn't just exist from season to season but communities of people who were all plugged into the *zoe* life that the gospel provides. Like their fathers in the faith, these churches would turn the world upside-down for the glory of God. I want this for myself, and I hope you do too.

When it comes to living the cross-shaped gospel—a *zoe* life of significance that both worships God and helps those around us—most Christians

> What we need is a two-part gospel. We need to serve God and our fellow man.

are only halfway there. One part of the church of Jesus Christ has removed the horizontal beam of the cross and focused solely on the vertical—their relationship with God. Others who claim to love Jesus have detached the vertical beam, focusing instead on the horizontal beam—their relationship with others. Like a surgeon with an injured hand, both sides have discovered that their ability to engage their world for the glory of God has been severely impaired.

What we need is a two-part gospel—a holistic gospel, a gospel that loves both the Father and His Son, the Redeemer Jesus, and at the same time declares that love as it seeks the souls of the lost. We need to serve God and our fellow man. We need that two-part harmony!

Where Did We Go Wrong?

If asked to present the gospel, how would you go about that? When I'm asked to give the gospel, someone expects me to give a clear presentation followed by an invitation for people to accept Jesus Christ as their Lord and Savior. Now, I don't want to diminish this at all. In fact, the apostle Paul says that this is of first importance (1 Corinthians 15:3). Our soul's deepest longing is to be in relationship with God.

However, what I want to suggest is that this is not *all* that is meant by the gospel in the Scriptures. Jesus, Paul, and the other apostles knew that the gospel had profound social implications as well, creating bold new paradigms for both how people related to one another and how they engaged their world as well. Yet church history has revealed that the force of the gospel has been severely blunted, and lives negatively impacted when we have divorced the horizontal dimensions of the gospel (our need to love and engage others) from the vertical (our need to love and engage God through His Son, Jesus Christ). Unfortunately, this separation has become the norm. It was Charles Spurgeon who once said that "One recurring tragedy of the Christian church . . . has been the separation of social ministries and spiritual, evangelistic ministries."[3]

George Whitefield and the Gospel

One of the greatest proclaimers of the gospel in church history was the English evangelist George Whitefield. Before Billy Graham, it can be argued that no one preached the gospel in America and the United Kingdom to more people than Whitefield in the eighteenth century and D. L. Moody in the nineteenth century. Whitefield's influence on how we view the gospel today is both positive and negative.

Possessed with Spirit-given abilities, Whitefield's spellbinding dominance over his audience was such that masses of people flocked to hear him. In fact, so many people came that he could no longer preach in church buildings; he had to take to the fields. Over the span of his ministry, it is estimated that he preached over eighteen thousand times[4] to millions of people. A person of his stature would go down as one of the greatest men God has ever used, but at the same time there was a severe blemish on his earthly record.

George Whitefield owned slaves. To be sure, he was not the only preacher of his time to do so. Jonathan Edwards, a man called America's greatest theologian, did as well. What makes Whitefield stand out, though, is that it was because of this preacher of the gospel's influence that Georgia legalized slavery. Using his friendship with General James Oglethorpe, founder of the colony of Georgia, Whitefield lobbied to have slavery legalized. In a letter written to Oglethorpe and the trustees of the Colony of Georgia, Whitefield pleaded his case:

"My chief end in writing this, is to inform you . . . that I am as willing as ever to do all I can for Georgia and the Orphan House, if either a limited use of negroes is approved of, or some more indented servants [are] sent over. If not, I cannot promise to keep any large family, or cultivate the plantation in any considerable manner."[5]

Whitefield's biographer, Arnold Dallimore, remarks at the close of this letter, "Such was Whitefield's urging of the Trustees to allow slavery in Georgia, and as stated earlier, we can but deplore both his attitude and his action. . . . In 1750 the British Government submitted to the wishes of the majority of the people of Georgia; Oglethorpe's slaveless society was done away with and slavery was made a legal practice in the colony."[6]

Tim Keller reminds us that we must always look for the sin beneath the sin, and when we examine George Whitefield's desire to have slavery legalized in Georgia, we are forced to conclude that racism is not the ultimate issue. No, there's a far greater problem. What kind of gospel did Whitefield preach that would allow the proclamation of Jesus Christ to millions of people—a man who died because God so loved the world— to coexist with lobbying for the legalization of slavery? Whitefield's problem was not a race problem; it was a gospel problem. Whatever he may have purported to believe about the gospel, or to have preached, what is obvious for Whitefield is that in practice he understood the gospel to be almost solely in terms of my relationship with Christ to the exclusion of my relationship with others.

In fairness, Whitefield did preach to the slaves, which in that day was not very common, for it was thought among many white Christians that they did not have souls and were therefore not worthy of preaching to. Whitefield disagreed. And certainly God used many other deeply flawed Christian leaders. Yet Whitefield—and many believers to this day—compartmentalized the gospel, emphasizing salvation while neglecting God's call to care for those in need.

Billy Graham Leads the Way

Billy Graham, the greatest evangelist of the twentieth century, understood the importance of preaching a gospel for all people. While some early crusades in the South were segregated, Graham quickly came to see that God wanted the walls between the races torn down—literally and figuratively. On March 15, 1953, just a few days into his crusade meetings in Chattanooga, Tennessee, he personally removed the ropes that separated the black and white sections of the audience. One year later, after the US Supreme Court ruled (in *Brown v. the Board of Education*) that separate schools for blacks and whites were unconstitutional, he began to practice integration, both in his crusades and on the platform. His crusade team included a preacher from India and later an African-American associate evangelist, Howard Owen Jones.[7] Yet his emphasis was not civil rights but the gospel itself, that people would find salvation through Christ: "The ground at the foot of the cross is level, and it touches my heart when I see whites standing shoulder to shoulder with blacks at the cross."[8] Unfortunately, much of the evangelical church lagged behind Billy Graham in those days.

> Billy Graham personally removed the ropes that separated black and white sections of the audience.

Jesus and the Gospel

Like the evangelists of the last three centuries, we must be careful to retain the gospel as presented by Jesus Christ. In Matthew 4, Jesus is facing hordes of people, all trying to get this new miracle worker's attention. He calls upon them to "Repent, for the kingdom of heaven is at hand" (4:17). Clearly, this is Jesus appealing for all to turn from their sins and follow Him. Repentance, as Jesus defined it and the likes of Whitefield and Finney understood it, was the need to surrender your heart to God and live a radically different life. But notice what happens next:

> And he went throughout all Galilee, teaching in their synagogues and proclaiming the *gospel* of the kingdom and healing every disease and every affliction among the people. So his fame spread throughout all Syria, and they brought him all the sick, those afflicted with various diseases and pains, those oppressed by demons, epileptics, and paralytics, and he healed them. (4:23–25, emphasis added)

Later on in chapter 9, Matthew would note the same thing about the ministry of Jesus:

> And Jesus went throughout all the cities and villages, teaching in their synagogues and proclaiming the *gospel* of the kingdom and healing every disease and every affliction. When he saw the crowds, he had compassion for them, because they were harassed and helpless, like sheep without a shepherd. (35–36, emphasis added)

Both passages intentionally say the same thing. No communicator repeats without wanting to drive home a point. In these two passages, Matthew is grabbing our collars, wanting us to understand something very important about the ministry of Jesus.

That is: *Jesus aids the oppressed and afflicted as well.* In other words, the gospel according to Jesus is spiritual with physical implications; it attends to both the needs of the soul and the needs of the body.

"You Feed Them"

In the middle of Matthew 14, Jesus is attracting a huge crowd, and many are seeking healing. The crowd is hungry, and the disciples petition Jesus to send them away so they can get their own food. Jesus, the one who should most be weary of the crowd, tells the disciples that they need to feed them. He orders the crowd to sit down, and taking five loaves of bread and two pieces of fish, He feeds them. As thousands finish their meal, Jesus slips out the back, hops in a boat, and takes off, with not one word being said.

Not one stanza of *Just as I Am* is sung. No one comes to the altar for salvation, because no one's been asked. But if I discard my twenty-first-century evangelical understanding of the gospel and look at it through the lens of Jesus, I'm forced to conclude that Christ's feeding the thousands who were gathered that day was very much a part, a demonstration if you will, of the gospel.

Something in us is uncomfortable with this. We want to call this social justice or compassion ministry. However, the model Jesus leaves is that the kingdom of heaven exists to bring order to chaos—to transform lives, spiritually and physically. This is the gospel in action.

> The gospel according to Jesus attends to both the needs of the soul and the needs of the body.

Paul: Reworking Relationships

Outside of Jesus Christ, no one had more influence on the trajectory of Christianity in its formative years than the apostle Paul. Writer of close to half the New Testament and planter of many churches, his fingerprints on the church can still be felt. Study the ministry of Paul and you find something curious. Whenever he comes to town he always asks two questions: (1) Where's the local synagogue? and (2) Where do the Gentiles hang out? He wanted to spend time with these two groups of people who wouldn't dare do life with one another. Paul would begin by preaching to the Jews, and then he would spend a lot of time preaching to Gentiles. If he's in Ephesus he goes to the lecturew hall of Tyrannus to find the Gentiles (Acts 19:9), or in Athens he's at Mars Hill (Acts 17:22).

By going to both the Jews and the Gentiles, Paul eventually faced a challenge. Some Jews would convert to Christianity and so would some Gentiles. But now what? Does he start a church for the Jews on the north side of town and a separate church for the Gentiles on the south side? This makes sense, especially when you consider that the social norms of the day meant that Jews and Gentiles just didn't mix—it was too messy, especially for the Jews and all their dietary and ceremonial standards. The easy and most efficient thing to do, most could argue, was to keep them segregated.

The last thing you would want to do is to push against the social norms, but Paul's understanding of the gospel wouldn't let him take the easy way out. So, making an extreme break with the cultural customs of the day, Paul put these new Jewish and Gentile converts to Christianity in one church and challenged them to do life together and to love one another.

There were some obstacles along the way. Like when a Gentile family would invite a Jewish family over to their house for dinner, and the sheer horror on the Jewish family's face when a half a rack of ribs was placed on their plates. Paul deals with this in places like Romans 14. Or, what does one do when a group of Jews start making Gentiles feel bad for not being circumcised? Paul would have to double back and address this culturally messy issue in the book of Galatians. Paul would be the first to tell you that there are a lot of headaches when you start pushing against the social and cultural norms. But he would also say that it's worth it. Our new-found love for Jesus demands a reworking of relationships.

The Bible on Class Differences

Looking back on it, Korie and I both agree that our first date was *miserable*. I would say that part of the reason for the debacle was that she talked a whole lot. She'd answer, "Well, that's what happens when you're asked questions about yourself the whole time." The next time I took her out, I chose a place where she wouldn't talk so much. A place where I could quietly adore her. We ended up at the movie theater.

It was spring of 1998, and I knew that the perfect movie to take her to was the James Cameron film *Titanic*. For over three hours we sat quietly and soaked in the love story of Jack and Rose, the most unlikely of couples. In an era where the social norms deeply divided the haves from the have-nots, Jack found his way out of third class to the dinner table with Rose in first class. At the end of the meal, Rose sneaks across the divide, down to a beer-soaked party in steerage where the romance between the vagabond Jack and the high society Rose blossoms. As their love grows, the two begin to push harder against the social norms of the day, longing to experience a new paradigm in their relationship. Jack goes to his death refusing to accept the fact that poor must stay with poor and rich with rich.

The movie and my time with Korie were special, but the message of class division should not be ignored. Some historians suggest that the sinking of the *Titanic* represented the end of the Edwardian age—a period marked by insurmountable class divisions. The Bible, however, and the ministry of Paul proclaimed the death of class, race, and gender divisions centuries before the *Titanic* ended up at the bottom of the Atlantic.

To the believers who lived in Galatia and to all who read his epistle, he wrote:

For in Christ Jesus you are all sons of God, through faith. For as many of you as were baptized into Christ have put on Christ. There is neither Jew nor Greek, there is neither slave nor free, there is no male and female, for you are all one in Christ Jesus. And if you are

Christ's, then you are Abraham's offspring, heirs according to the promise. (Galatians 3:26–29)

In his short letter to Philemon, Paul appealed to the wealthy slave owner to receive back his once fugitive slave as a "beloved brother" (verse 16). He instructed Gentile believers to recognize that Christ had "broken down in his flesh the dividing wall of hostility" so they could reconcile with their Jewish brothers (Ephesians 2:14).

Jews and Gentiles United by the Cross

Paul uses the term *Gentiles* a lot in his letters. When he does, he always uses the term in one of two ways: (1) spiritually, in describing people who don't know Jesus Christ; or (2) ethnically, to speak of non-Jews. In the Ephesians 2 passage (listed above), we see that he uses the term *Gentiles* ethnically, because he says in verse 11, "Gentiles in the flesh." I bring this up because what follows in the Ephesians 1 passage is really insightful about how Paul understood the gospel and its impact in how we are to relate to one another.

As divided as Jews and Gentiles were in the ancient world, the Jews did allow the Gentiles to come and worship at the temple. One of the qualifications for Gentiles who wanted to worship the God of the Jews was that they did so in one specific area—the Court of the Gentiles. This was a section of the temple that not only was reserved for them but also divided them from the three other courts where Jews were allowed to go and worship. In fact, there were signs on the walls in the Court of the Gentiles that informed these Jewish sympathizers that if they ventured beyond the walls, they would be killed. Paul, in writing to the Ephesians, a multiethnic church composed of Jews and Gentiles, uses temple wording. The phrase "dividing wall of hostility" was taken from the temple, and specifically the wall that separated the Gentiles from the other areas of the temple.

The bad news is that before Jesus Christ, the Gentiles were separated and alienated from "the commonwealth of Israel." The good news, however, is that because of what Christ has accomplished on the cross, when He died in our place and for our sins, the dividing wall of hostility has been removed.

This, according to Paul, has profound relational implications, because now Jew and Gentile can worship together as one! Paul sees the gospel as providing *both* our reconciliation to God and our reconciliation to one another! To Paul, the gospel was both vertical and horizontal.

Dinner Tables and Unlikely Friends

When a couple gets married, there is at the same time a necessary re-patterning of relationships. The image that comes to mind is that of a dinner table, where the families of both sides have left their previous dinner tables to sit at one new table. The question now becomes, where do both sides sit? This is a great question for the bride, whose father once sat at the head of the table up until the point she said, "I do." Now, because of the marriage covenant, the dad, though still very much a part of her life, must now change seats, allowing the husband to occupy this place. The same is true for the husband. While his mother may have sat opposite from the head of the table in a seat of authority for much of his life, Mama must now make some adjustments, if the new marriage is going to thrive. Fail to make these shifts at the "dinner table" of marriage, and you will have a lot of problems. The covenant of marriage demands a drastic new paradigm in how we approach relationships.

This is what Paul is getting at when talking about the covenant between a believer and Christ. Before we fell in love with Jesus, we were seated at the head of our own tables. For some, prior to Jesus, they may have lived naturally segregated lives, where the maxim "birds of a feather flock together" was true of them. But now, having entered the marriage covenant with Christ, they are seated at the multiethnic, multisocioeconomic dinner table of the church, where Christ is the new head. Now

> Paul knew the challenges that the gospel presented in overturning old relationship paradigms.

they are told to do life with one another, to love one another, serve one another, and encourage one another. The covenant of salvation demands a radical re-patterning of relationships.

In Galatians 2, Paul rehearses a troubling scene. The apostle Peter used to do dinner with the Gentiles, which for a Jew was no small thing. Then his Jewish buddies started to come around, and Peter retreated back into old relationship patterns by withdrawing from the Gentiles and hanging out with only the Jews. Paul, also a Jewish man, was ticked, to say the least, and he confronts Peter. In the heat of the conversation Paul lets it be known that Peter was "not living up to the truth of the Gospel" (2:14 AMP). For Peter to not walk in a new relationship by coming to the dinner table with his Gentile brothers and sisters in Christ was a gross failure to understand and apply the gospel.

Paul knew the challenges that the gospel presented in overturning old relationship paradigms and introducing new ones. Though Peter was considered the apostle to the Gentiles, motivated by the vision from God and a meeting with the Gentile centurion Cornelius (Acts 10), Paul would spend time with Gentiles as well. He brought his Gentile buddy Trophimus to Jerusalem, and a riot ensued after certain Jews falsely accused him of bringing Trophimus into the inner portion of the temple (Acts 21:27–32). Paul is arrested, and the rest of his life in the book of Acts is spent in the custody of others. Paul's friendships with the Gentiles pushed against the social norms of his day.

My best friend growing up was black like me. Even though we shared the same race, we were as different as Colin Powell and Tupac Shakur. I was the Theo Huxtable to his Allen Iverson. He lived on a dead-end street in the projects, while my street had a cul-de-sac. His dad was never around; my dad led us in prayer around the dinner table. He was on the reduced lunch plan at school and rode the bus. I drove to school and had my own bank account.

As different as we were, our friendship has lasted over thirty years. One of the main reasons for this is that my parents fought to make sure that we were always around each other. When my father wanted to take me to a ballgame, he got an extra ticket for my friend so he could come along. When my parents were concerned about my spiritual life and wanted to send me to some youth conference, they made sure my friend came too by paying his registration fee; they even gave him spending money.

By no stretch of the imagination are my parents wealthy, but they do represent the middle-class African-American demographic that began life in a lower class. In his book *Our Kind of People*, Lawrence Graham notes how, once out of the hood, the African-American middle to upper middle classes do not even think of reaching back to befriend, much less help those left behind. The gospel of Jesus Christ, however, compelled my parents to blow up old paradigms and to invite people of different classes to their dinner table.

Movie Messages

Think of the movies that you find most compelling, that move you, that even make you cry. For me, in most cases those movies involve people coming together and doing life who absolutely should not be at the dinner table together. It's me bawling my eyes out as I watch again *Schindler's List*, witnessing the kindness and compassion of a German man named Oskar Schindler toward abused Jews. Or it's that scene in *Remember the Titans*, when the white quarterback from California named Sunshine tries to knock down the segregated norms of the South by walking into a burger joint after a football game with some of his black friends. In both examples can be found the treasure of the gospel. Before Oskar and Sunshine stepped across the divide, Jesus left heaven and came to earth. He sat at the dinner table with prostitutes and tax collectors. He pushed against social norms by sitting in public with a woman at the well. When society said lepers were to be out on the fringes of the community, He touched them. When a Gentile woman came begging for "crumbs" from the table, Jesus provided for her. Through it all, Jesus overturned the old dinner table and left us a new one, filled with rich and poor, Jews and Gentiles, slave and free. Along the way, people were either in awe or wanted to kill Him, because to see Jesus and how He related to others was to see a completely new way. To some it was the way it shouldn't be, but to Jesus it was exactly the way it was supposed to be.

Life with Jesus is not only about a quiet time in the morning, with a Bible on your lap and a cup of coffee in your hand. As important as it is to study God's Word, the gospel must launch us out to question and push against the unbiblical social norms of our world in a redemptive way. Only then have we truly understood what it means to follow Jesus.

2 REACHING OUT BY FIRST REACHING UP

The modern liberal Church is fond of appealing
to experience. But where shall true Christian
experience be found if not in the blessed
peace which comes from Calvary?[1]

J. Gresham Machen

Many of us know people we love who aren't living according to God's design. Perhaps they're cohabiting, or have had an abortion, or are getting a divorce. We love them. We love God—and His standard for holiness. What to do?

Most Christians, when making the hard choices in honoring God and honoring people, decide between two operating systems: (1) Either we filter people's experience through God's Word, or (2) we filter God's Word through people's experience. This is problematic, because we seem to be pitting love for God against love for neighbor, which is a distinction the Bible never makes.

Quiet Accomplices?

As I emphasized in chapter 1, the gospel includes both our vertical relationship with God and our horizontal relationship with others. Our relationship with God is always first. You can't reach out without first reaching up. But once you reach up to the Savior—or He reaches out to you—the response to His grace is to reach out to your neighbor. We cannot ignore our neighbor. In fact, we make the gospel appealing to our neighbors and the world by our acts of compassion.

We've already looked at how the church in recent centuries, while she has expressed a profound love for God as seen in her commitment to the authority of Scripture has often not gone far enough by letting her love for God leak out into love for others in ways that would challenge the unjust sociological structures of our society. In fact, the church's historic failure to live out the horizontal dimensions of the gospel has at the same time made Christians quiet accomplices to such sociological injustices as classism, racism, and sexism (more on those three beginning in the next chapter).

Noted American historian George Marsden summed up the sentiment of the church when it came to issues of loving one's neighbor, what many might call, pejoratively, the "social gospel." Marsden points out that the mindset of some believers for much of the twentieth century "suggested that Christian political efforts were largely futile. Believers . . . should separate into pure churches and preach the gospel for the higher cause that eternal souls would be saved for eternity. [Advocates say:] 'Why try to clean up the staterooms of the *Titanic* when you know she is doomed?' "[2] During the second half of the twentieth century, a new view emerged called progressive dispensationalism, which proposes that the church must engage society even as she awaits Christ's return.[3]

Clearly portions of theological systems about the future kingdom leave the unsettling impression that we can overlook the issues of our society. Since the earth is headed for destruction, as the argument goes, we should not focus on the physical/social needs of people; instead, focus on the soul. This perspective ignores the Jesus of the Gospels, who fed and healed people more times than He preached to them a sermon.

First: Love God

In Matthew 22 Jesus is asked a tough question: Which is the greatest commandment? When there are over six hundred choices (laws) to pick from, we can see that this posed a seemingly impossible dilemma. If it were me, I probably would have stuck with any of the Ten Commandments, maybe narrowing it down to the first one just to play it safe. Surprisingly, Jesus doesn't play it safe. In typical fashion Jesus takes the atypical route:

And he said to him, "You shall love the Lord your God with all your heart and with all your soul and with all your mind. This is the great and first commandment. And a second is like it: You shall love your neighbor as yourself. On these two commandments depend all the Law and the Prophets." (Matthew 22:37–49)

Jesus whittles the whole law down to two great commandments: love for God and love for neighbor. Here we find Jesus simplifying Christianity to our vertical relationship with God and our horizontal relationship with others. Jesus goes on to say that the whole law fits into these two commands. Notice the order of Jesus' response. The first command is to love God; the second is to love our neighbor. Both of these laws make up the essential DNA of any Christ-follower. But they're not equal. Loving God must be first, and our obligation to love our neighbor must be seen through the lens of our love for God.

> Loving God must be first, and our obligation to love our neighbor must be seen through the lens of our love for God.

What exactly does it mean to love God? Jesus sheds light on this when He says that we are to love God with "all of [our] mind." John Piper, in his book *Think: The Life of the Mind and the Love of God*, argues that our thoughts are vital in shaping our affections for God. The source for thinking rightly about God, and therefore loving Him, is the Word of God. So one of the ways we love God is allowing the Word of God to shape our minds and inform our thoughts about Him.

The latter half of Psalm 19 is a beautiful picture of God's Word. Drawing from his own experience, David says that the Word of God *restores the soul, rejoices the heart, enlightens the eyes,* and is to therefore be *desired* more than anything in this world. As the reader finishes this text, he's forced to conclude that the Bible is not some stale piece of ancient literature, but is a sacred gift bequeathed to us to stir our love for God. To love God is to love His truth, His Word. When we love God and His Word, this becomes the standard by which we are able to navigate how to love our neighbors.

Intimate abiding relationships are built on the premise of a mutual commitment to some standard of truth. Korie and I have enjoyed more than a decade of marriage because we run on the same operating system—a love for God. We've remained faithful to one another because of our faithfulness to God. When we've gotten cross with one another and said or done things we shouldn't have, our commitment to a God who forgives us and calls us to forgive one another, not returning evil for evil, is what drives us to say, "I'm sorry." When the turmoils of life crashed into our marriage through seasons of miscarriage, financial difficulties, and sickness, our love for God weathered the storm. Our love for God tethers us together and helps us to traverse the journey of marriage in a God-honoring way. The covenant of marriage has shown Korie and me that we can't fulfill the second great commandment to love each other without fulfilling the first—loving God.

Relationships are strengthened when there is a greater commitment to something or Someone greater than the relationship. Without this suprarelational commitment, community becomes at best shallow, and isolation is soon to follow. We see this in our culture. Many suffer from acute loneliness. While isolation has plagued humankind throughout history because of the sinful effects of the fall, it seems as if the problem has only intensified. The experts point to a number of factors—the rise of social networks and its downside of presenting a mirage of intimacy, video games replacing being with our neighbors, even the demise of front porches where people greeted people. I'm sure there's some truth in these reasons, but could it be that the spike in isolation and loneliness runs parallel to the idol of relativism in our society in which each man does what is right in his own eyes? With the demise of truth has come the unraveling of relationships.

The Liberal Church and Loving Our Neighbor

I don't like labels, and I especially don't like the term *liberal*. One of the definitions for *liberal* in the *Random House Webster's College Dictionary* is, "characterized by generosity and willingness to give in large amounts." By that definition we should all be liberal—liberal with our time, our money, our gifts.

But there's another, less positive definition of *liberal*. In reference to the church, the term describes a historical departure among a group of churches from the basic tenets of the faith, while strongly emphasizing active social involvement. For much of the early decades of the twentieth century, what has been called the fundamentalist-modernist controversy dominated the American religious landscape. While that history is not crucial to this book, we should note that at the center of the controversy was a debate over the gospel. Is the gospel a set of beliefs (what some would call fundamentals), or is it social action? To frame the question another way: Is the gospel my vertical relationship with God as seen in my commitment to His Word, or is it my horizontal relationship with others?

The liberal church today might well be described as elevating the command to love our neighbor over the command to love God with the totality of our being. (I know that any person attending a liberal church would naturally say that he or she loves God, but the liberal church exists because of a choice, in part, to elevate love for neighbor over a love for God as seen in a commitment to love God's Word.)

During my midtwenties, some leaders of a church invited me to candidate for the position of senior pastor. Encouraged by my mentors who thought the process would be good for me, and seeing the redemptive potential of visiting that church, I agreed. As my sweaty palms gripped the side of the podium that first Sunday morning, I was surprised to see that no one had brought their Bibles. At the end of my message, I was welcomed with great affection and immediately invited back to preach another sermon. One person even tried to move to vote me in on the spot.

My excitement that day began to wane when I was greeted by a middle-aged man still wearing his choir robe. After he finished his complimentary remarks, he asked me if I would be willing to officiate the union of his homosexual partner and him. Shocked, I put on my best poker face and gave some political answer, making a note to bring that up with the search committee the next time we met. When I shared this with the committee, their response was that they were an open and affirming church, which meant that they approved of the homosexual lifestyle, and anyone who wished to serve as their senior pastor needed to be on the same page. Careful not to reveal my hand just yet, I probed them for their theological justification. At the end of the discussion it was obvious that their "love for neighbor" was the greatest command, if not the only.

My short-lived candidacy at this church was an eye-opening experience. Older members had been on the front lines of the Civil Rights Movement. Yet with no suprarelational commitment to guide them, without a Truth compass, they fell deeper and deeper into heresy. At some point loving God was sacrificed on the altar of loving one's neighbor, and in the process they failed at both.

Right Beliefs = Right Behavior

Without that compass, any behavior can be regarded as right behavior. But right behavior comes about only by right beliefs—beliefs based on the truth.

Part of the tension comes because some Christians see a belief system or a set of creedal pronouncements as arbitrary or secondary. They may even want to discard the creeds as unnecessary or divisive.

In his book *The Future of Faith*, Harvard Divinity School professor Harvey Cox argues that Christianity is not to be reduced to a set of creeds, but must be displayed through the actions of the professed follower of Jesus. Any Jesus lover could agree with Cox. The problem comes when Dr. Cox seems to flirt with wanting to dismantle the entire belief system. He writes:

Once I realized that Christianity is not a creed and that faith is more a matter of embodiment than of axioms, things changed. I began to look at people I met in a new way. Some of the ones I admired most were "believers" in the conventional sense, but others were not. . . . This suggested to me just how mistaken conventional belief-oriented Christianity is in the way it separates the sheep from the goats. But then according to the Gospel of Matthew (25:31–46) Jesus also rejects this predictable schema. What he said then no doubt shocked his listeners. He insisted that those who are welcomed into the Kingdom of God—those who were clothing the naked, feeding the hungry, and visiting the prisoners—were not "believers" and were not even aware that they had been practicing the faith he was teaching and exemplifying.[4]

I share Harvey Cox's frustration with so-called followers of Jesus Christ who can argue fine points of doctrine yet do not allow the gospel to push them into uncomfortable waters by way of lifestyle. But Dr. Cox

> Right beliefs are vital for fueling right behavior.

has overreacted. Right beliefs are vital for fueling right behavior. This is a lesson I learned on my very first day in seminary when Dr. Holloman asked my incoming class which was more important—orthodoxy (right beliefs) or orthopraxy (right practice). Sitting in my small group as we tried to pick this question apart, the word we kept coming back to was "right." Anyone can do charitable deeds, but if we defined "right" in the greater context of that which gives God glory, and ultimately builds our neighbor up, then we could not separate orthopraxy from orthodoxy. We were forced to conclude that *both* are essential. When love for neighbor (orthopraxy) is stripped away from love for God (orthodoxy), I will eventually fail to genuinely love my neighbor, because at some point I will define my love for them based on either what I think is best, or what they think is best, not what God deems as best.

When We Ignore the Fences of Truth

Some years ago a story ran in the newspapers of a young teenage boy whose hat had blown off of a roller coaster at an amusement park. He must've really loved this hat because he was obsessed with getting it back. The problem was that there were huge fences and signs that prohibited him and others from getting close to the roller coaster. Ignoring these rules, he scaled the fence. He was on the track, about to get the hat, when the roller coaster came racing through and killed him. Reading this story, I was forced to conclude that the roller coaster didn't kill him as much as his love for his hat.

The problem with the liberal church is that in her quest to love her neighbor she has ignored the fences of God's truth; in the process her effectiveness has been greatly harmed. What's true of the church is true of the people who subscribe to this same warped perspective of love. Patting someone on the back and telling them that their lifestyle choices are fine as long as it makes them happy will not transform them nor our society, much less get them to heaven.

The Standard of Truth: That Vertical Beam

Jesus did not love His neighbor detached from any standard of truth. His love for neighbor was filtered through a love for God. Consider these passages:

Of a prostitute who came weeping at His feet, Jesus said: "Your sins are forgiven. . . . Your faith has saved you; go in peace.'" (Luke 7:48, 50)

The woman at the well said of her conversation with Jesus: "Come, see a man who told me all that I ever did." (John 4:29)

Of a woman caught in adultery: "Jesus stood up and said to her, 'Woman, where are they? Has no one condemned you?' She said, 'No one, Lord.' And Jesus said, 'Neither do I condemn you; go, and from now on sin no more.'" (John 8:10–11)

The power of the gospel only happens when we, the bride of Christ, love God with our total being. This is the reason we must always draw close to God, for it is only by reaching upward that we can reach outward in power and with the proper motives.

A group of about thirty people from our church under the direction of careful experts invited me one Saturday to help them build a home in an impoverished community. I'm no expert—my part was to hammer some nails—but watching the building process was a real eye-opener. By the time we had arrived, the experts had already poured the concrete foundation, and we were ready to start erecting the frame of the house. The frame was primarily made up of a series of long vertical beams. Once these studs were in place, we then nailed rectangular sheets of wood to these wooden beams to stabilize the frame. These inner walls would be vital to the home's strength. It didn't take a genius to figure out why we framed the house in this order: vertical first and then horizontal. We had to begin with the vertical pieces of wood because without it the horizontal wood sheets were useless. There had to be something to nail these pieces to, to provide a stable structure for years to come.

The cross that Jesus died on was also composed of the vertical and horizontal. While both pieces are necessary, the vertical beam is primary, because this is the piece that provides the foundation. The vertical beam was rooted firmly in the ground. Without it, the horizontal beam was useless.

Yes, both elements of the cross-shaped gospel—my relationship with God and my relationship with others—are necessary. However, the vertical dimension of the gospel—the fact that God has redeemed us by the blood of His Son, Jesus, and has adopted us into His family—is primary. Without a vertical relationship with God, our horizontal relationships with others are devoid both of power and any eternal meaning.

The Power of the First Commandment To Free Us to Serve

What's striking about the three Gospel passages above (and others too) is that Jesus shows incredible love for His neighbor within the supra-relational structure of the first and greatest commandment. He doesn't just pat them on the back and display "love." Quite the opposite—in each case He alludes to their sin. Had Jesus operated by the liberal and post-modern understanding of love, there would have been no need for the cross. Why die on one, when no one is willing to say they are in error?

The incredible power of Jesus' ministry is seen in His uncanny ability to attract sinners, famous sinners at that, and to transform their lives not by a blind love that refused to see their sins but by pointing out their sins yet releasing them in grace and forgiveness. This is what it genuinely means to love one's neighbor. The power of the gospel, and the source of the church's effectiveness, only happens when we, the bride of Christ, love God with our total being. Then we have the power to serve in love. It is then that we will be equipped to call people to a standard of living and love them beautifully to the awe of the world and the glory of God.

3 DONKEYS AND ELEPHANTS

We are not a triumphant theocratic nation dwelling
in an earthly holy land, but a band of dispossessed
pilgrims whose true country—of which Eden and Canaan
were types and shadows—is not to be found
"under the sun" but beyond it, in heaven itself.[1]

Jason J. Stellman

I was never in more need of some Advil than in the fall of 2008 when the presidential elections were reaching their climax. Many of the African Americans in our church were unashamed to broadcast their excitement for Democratic candidate Barack Obama. One woman even wanted me to grant her permission to sell "Yes We Can" T-shirts after service.

At the same time many of our white members were put off by what they considered to be reverse racism, when they realized that one of the main reasons many of our African-American members were voting for Obama was the simple fact that they shared the same racial heritage. Conversely, I had just finished shaking hands at the end of one service, as I did every Sunday, and had started walking up the aisle when I saw a white gentleman running toward me. By the time he reached me, he was almost breathless, but once he shook my hand, he placed a McCain/Palin campaign button in my palm. He asked if I could announce at the last minute that anyone who wanted one could come down front and see him.

We used to do something at our church called ERACE groups. Over a six-week period we would pull together twelve people—six white, six black, placing them all in this group. Each group met weekly in someone's home to look at their attitudes and align them with Scriptures as they sought to uncover and eradicate—*erase*—racism in their hearts. The first week each person would write several questions anonymously and place them in a bowl, and for the rest of our time the questions in this bowl served as our curriculum. We weren't looking to solve the problems of the world, or even to come up with the "right" answers to the questions; we were just trying to create some dialogue, and hopefully form some cross-cultural relationships.

You sit in enough of these groups, as Korie and I have, and you find out that most of the questions are pretty much the same: Why do black preachers drive Cadillacs? Isn't affirmative action unfair? Why were whites so sad when O. J. Simpson got off? Why were blacks so happy? Why are middle-class whites often Republican? Why are blacks Democrat? The question of politics and race usually bleeds over into a discussion of economics. Your poorer demographic will typically gravitate toward Democrat, while the wealthy toward Republican. It's never that nice and neat, but it is close enough.

Hearing the discussions that take place in these ERACE groups, we figure out that the issue of politics, race, and economics are intertwined. In fact, if you were to hop in the car with me as we cruised down the streets of Memphis, I could point out to you the churches where Democrats feel at home and the ones where they do not. Without fail, if it's wealthy and white, leave the Obama T-shirts in the car; but if it's middle to lower-middle class and black, feel free to wear those shirts. The mind-blowing thing about our church, Fellowship Memphis, is that no political label fits us. Because we're racially diverse, we're at the same time economically and politically diverse as well.

So when the requests came in to distribute the Obama T-shirts and the McCain buttons, something needed to be said. For me, the challenge was never about creating a safe place for both groups to coexist. Cultivating a middle-ground culture, where lovers of both Fox and MSNBC News could mingle, took a distant backseat to cultivating a gospel culture.

I needed to see what Jesus and the gospel had to say about the issues of *politics*, *race*, and *economics*—three of the most volatile topics there are. As we explore what the gospel has to say about these subjects, my aim is not to take sides or to even establish a balance. It's simply to mine and extract from the Scriptures what the gospel requires of us as followers of Jesus.

Let's begin with the "safe" topic of politics.

Was Jesus a Revolutionary?

One of the chief expectations the Jews had of their Messiah was that he would be a political leader who would overthrow their oppressors and establish a new government that would not just be spiritual but would be physical as well. To be fair, I could see how they would assume this, especially when they read passages like the one in Isaiah 9 where it was prophesied of the Christ that the *government* would be on His shoulders (see verses 6–8). Given this expectation, when Jesus came claiming that He was the long-awaited Messiah, the Promised One, some Jews were waiting for Him to ignite a political revolution that would take direct aim at mighty Rome. When Jesus chose Simon the Zealot to be one of His disciples, their excitement spiked, because the Zealots were your revolutionaries, always ready at a moment's notice to rumble.

But just as quickly as their hopes arose, so they soon found themselves disappointed when a guy by the name of Matthew was selected. After all, Matthew, formerly known as Levi, was a Jewish tax collector, the cultural equivalent of an Uncle Tom, because he was a Jew collecting taxes at unjust rates from his Jewish brothers and sisters and taking part of those proceeds to help fund the very empire that was oppressing his people. Nothing was more reprehensible to Jews than a Jewish tax collector who had the audacity to work for "the man."

Those first couple of trips had to be pretty tense as Matthew the tax collector was walking through the fields alongside the likes of Simon the Zealot. For those outside of the group who got the chance to get to know these men, it would be a gross understatement to say that more than a few eyebrows were raised when they found out what these two did for a living prior to following Jesus.

What's more, the average Jew had to assume that there was no way Jesus could have been the Messiah, having a tax collector in His group, and going to parties where tax collectors fraternized with one another and Him. In the mind of the Jew, if one's going to start a political revolution, he needs to hang out with Simon's crowd, not Matthew's. But Jesus' political ambitions were a lot different from the expectations of His kinsmen.

The Hostile Religious Elite

When they could take it no longer, the now-hostile religious elite pressed the issue of politics with Jesus. The same Matthew who left his well-paying job to follow Jesus documents for us the tense exchange that follows:

Then the Pharisees went and plotted how to entangle him in his words. And they sent their disciples to him, along with the Herodians, saying, "Teacher, we know that you are true and teach the way of God truthfully, and you do not care about anyone's opinion, for you are not swayed by appearances. Tell us, then, what you think. Is it lawful to pay taxes to Caesar, or not?" But Jesus, aware of their malice, said, "Why put me to the test, you hypocrites? Show me the coin for the tax." And they brought him a denarius. And Jesus said to them, "Whose likeness and inscription is this?" They said, "Caesar's." Then he said to them, "Therefore render to Caesar the

things that are Caesar's, and to God the things that are God's."
When they heard it, they marveled. And they left him and went
away. (Matthew 22:15–22)

Matthew is careful to note by name the two groups of people who are
confronting Jesus: the Pharisees and the Herodians. While many of us see
the Pharisees as the self-righteous legalists of their day, loving rules more
than people, it's also important to know that they came from a sect of
Jews who vigorously opposed Rome. They picked a fight with the Romans
about two centuries before this exchange with Jesus. History would record
their skirmish with mighty Rome as the Maccabean Revolt. What's more
than clear, given their political position, is that the Pharisees were on the
side of *not* paying taxes to Caesar.

We also see another group in our passage called the Herodians. Like
the Pharisees they were also Jewish, but this is where the similarities stop.
The Herodians were a group of Jews who were loyal to King Herod. Rome
had allowed the Jews to experience a tiny measure of power by designat-
ing their own kings who were clearly subservient to Caesar and Rome.
Because of this the Herodians knew not to bite the hand that fed them and
were by default loyal to Rome and Caesar. We catch glimpses of the relationship between the Jewish king and the Roman powers when Jesus is
brought to trial before the Roman governor Pilate, who then sends Him
to Herod, hoping that Herod would settle the matter. Given the fact that
the Herodians did not want to rock the boat with Rome, they would have
been clearly on the side of paying taxes.

The Tie That Binds—Power

Make no mistake, there is no sense of objectivity among the two
groups. Both sides have their own opinions on how things should work,
and specifically that agenda centers around the theme of *power*. The Pharisees want political power by having a Messiah who would overthrow the

current regime, while the Herodians want to maintain their own political power that has been rationed out to them (no matter how small that ration may be) by the very same government that the Pharisees seek to overthrow.

This is why the strands of politics, race, and economics will forever be bound to each other, because the tie that binds is the question of power. We see this in our text where the freight trains of race, politics, and economics collide. Some of the Jewish race are questioning the perceived abuse by Gentiles (Rome). The Herodians represent an economically elite class of people, and the question being asked on the surface is one of politics, yet the underlying current to it all is power. If Jesus says they shouldn't pay taxes then He is affirming the Pharisees who long to exercise whatever power they have in acts of rebellion against Rome. But if Jesus says yes, that they should pay taxes, He is acknowledging the Herodian position and is okay with the status quo, which bows to Rome as the power structure of the day.

In the span of one chapter, we are not going to settle the issue of politics; that's not my aim. But we should be able to recognize that politics and power go hand in hand. Government can be an incredibly powerful force for good or evil, and the problem comes in defining what exactly is good and evil. Like the Pharisees and Herodians of Jesus' day, leaders today offer a myriad of opinions in how our government should exercise that power, with an equally wide selection of television channels devoted to voicing those opinions.

What's Your Agenda?

Some groups believe government should help the poor and bear the responsibility of providing health care for everyone who cannot afford it, while opening wide the borders to immigrants who want to leave their country and settle here. Specifically, they believe issues like health care and improving public education should be funded by the powerful (wealthy) through increased taxation. In other words, the government should flex its muscles and unleash its power toward the powerless.

For other groups, the issues are not that simple, especially if you have affluence and economic resources. At issue for this demographic is both the question of fairness and "rationality," for they argue that it is the powerful who have started the businesses and are keeping this country economically afloat, so why "bite the hand that feeds you"? Instead of a "big" government that is quick to bail some out, they advocate a "small" government that allows people to at least try and "pull themselves up by their bootstraps"; after all, isn't this the American way?

All this, plus Jesus' confrontation with the Pharisees and the Herodians, reveals that politics is never an objective thing. We all have our own agenda—right, wrong, or indifferent. I've never heard a poor person call President Obama a socialist, or an uninsured person wax eloquently on the evils of a government-subsidized health care plan. Coincidence?

Historically, African Americans in this country began as Republicans. If you think this is just happenstance, think again. It just so "happens" that the president who emancipated the slaves was a Republican named Lincoln. When the Great Depression hit some decades later and African Americans were especially affected, they began to lean toward the Democratic side of things, when the man in the office proposing a new deal was a Democrat named Roosevelt. And when African Americans were tired of living less than a human life in the Jim Crow South and beyond, who was it that signed the Civil and Voting Rights Acts? Many Democrats. What this brief trek through political history illustrates is that politics is never an objective thing. Whatever team lines up with *my* agenda (and certainly from the examples above we can admit that sometimes our agendas happen to be right) is what team I play for that season.

Today, the situation has changed for many African Americans, especially economically. While issues of poverty continue to plague minority communities, we are seeing the strengthening of an African-American middle- to upper-middle class. Being a part of this racial and economic demographic, I naturally have friends who traffic in the same circles. When we were talking about who we would vote for during the 2008 election, most of my friends said that either they were going to vote Republican, or were unsure about Barack Obama.

> We all must admit that no one walks into the voting booth completely objective.

Our economic stability has had an effect on how we approach the voting booth. Why is this, you may ask? The same way the wealthy tend to line up with any political team that is into small government, and shying away from heavily taxing the affluent—it fits our agenda. We all must admit that no one walks into the voting booth completely objective.

Who Are the Hypocrites?

The Pharisees and Herodians seem to have Jesus backed into a corner. After all, if Jesus says that we should pay taxes to Caesar, then He's just aligned Himself with the Herodians. If Jesus does this, He's hardly the political revolutionary that every Jew knew the Messiah would be. But on the other hand, if He says we shouldn't pay taxes to Caesar, He's just jumped on the backs of the Pharisees, while at the same time lining up against mighty Rome. For this well-known Rabbi to advocate not paying taxes to Caesar would at the same time be a declaration of war. He seems to have been backed into a corner with no way out.

Jesus now does something very curious—He calls them "hypocrites" while at the same time asking for the coin they use to pay the tax to Caesar. Just like that, these men dig through their personal possessions and someone hands over a coin. The coin in question has an image of Caesar on it. To the Pharisees, using this coin to pay taxes to Caesar promoted emperor worship. You would think if this was the position you held, that you wouldn't even want to carry the coin with you. But ironically, when Jesus calls for the coin in question, the very people who had these so-called convictions, the Pharisees, produce the coin. In other words, they had no problem using the coin to shop or to facilitate whatever kind of purposes they desired, yet the moment the coin didn't align with their likes or caused some discomfort, they all of a sudden had "convictions."

I love my Democratic brothers and sisters, many of whom chose that party because they are passionate about the poor (not to say Republicans are not). Their convictions find their place in the Scriptures, where over and over again God commands His people to engage the poor. Korie and I have this conviction, and if you're a follower of Jesus, so should you. But what I want to ask my Democratic neighbors is that if I took a peek at your tax statement, would I see a genuine commitment to the poor and less fortunate, or would I see someone who, like the Pharisees, talks a big game but doesn't genuinely and authentically live out their political declarations?

Many of my Republican friends are passionate about the issue of the right to life and speak out against abortion. This too is a deeply biblical conviction that we all should embrace as followers of Jesus. But if you'd forgive me, it's one thing to verbally speak out against the issue of abortion; it's a completely different thing to come alongside these young pregnant women and offer to foster or adopt. To simply articulate our belief in being pro-life but not even roll up our sleeves and offer positive alternatives is to play the part of hypocritic Pharisees. The easy thing is voting; the hard thing is being personally invested.

God and Government

Holding the coin in His hand, Jesus asks what appears to be a dumb question: "Whose likeness is on the coin?" I imagine the two groups shrugging their shoulders, turning up their palms, and tightening the skin on their foreheads as if to say, "Caesar, silly," while wondering if this was a trick question. Jesus returns the shrug of the shoulders by responding, "Well, pay taxes to him because it has his likeness on the coin." The Herodians think they've won.

Before the Herodians can celebrate, though, Jesus says, ". . . and to God the things that are God's." When Jesus says this both groups marvel, Matthew tells us, and then leave. Jesus gets out of the corner once again.

But wait a minute; what just happened? Living centuries later in a far distant land, we fail to see the beauty of Jesus' answer, but to a Jew they're in awe of the mastery of Christ.

In order to understand what has just occurred, we need to take a careful look at the word Jesus uses, "likeness." It is the Greek word *eikon*, and it simply means image. Both groups gathered that day with Jesus would have been more than familiar with the creation account of Genesis 1–2. It's here where God creates man in His image and likeness. In fact, the Greek translation of the Hebrew in Genesis has the word for image as "eikon." (This translation, known as the Septuagint, would have been around in Jesus' day.) So when Jesus uses the Hebrew word for *eikon*, these Jews could not help but think back to the creation where God makes man in His *eikon*.

As the logic goes, it's simple in Jesus' mind: give the government and Caesar their due; after all, it has his *eikon* on it, and because of that he owns it so return it to him. But then Jesus says we are to give to God what is God's. Well, what is God's? In context, *we* are God's! The totality of who we are belongs to Him because we have been made in His *eikon*, His image. Jesus is teaching that image equals ownership.

With one sentence Jesus has in essence said that their arguments about politics in the scheme of things are petty. Governments deal with aspects of our lives like currency (and others), while God wants all of our lives. Government, compared to the kingdom of God . . . well, there's no comparison.

Human governments are powerful but limited entities. They solely deal with the outward dimensions of our lives, not our hearts. Consider the outcome of the Civil Rights Movement—laws were changed. Because of Dr.

King and a host of others, I can now type these words from a nice hotel here in North Carolina, where I could never have stayed prior to the movement's efforts. I can buy property where I like, drink from any water fountain my heart desires, and sit in the front of the bus if I so choose.

> While government can change laws, it cannot change hearts.

So why am I still fighting against racial inequality and issues of economic injustice decades later? Because fundamentally these issues are not merely outward but inward; they stem from evil, fallen hearts. While government can change laws, it cannot change hearts. Her power is merely external and never internal.

The politics of Jesus seen through the gospel is counterintuitive to human government. Instead of working from the outside and trying to get in, the gospel begins on the inside and works itself out. Jesus is not anti-power; He just offers to us a radical new way of using that power. Jesus understood far too well that the most explosive use of power takes place when a tiny seed is planted in the hearts of humanity, and given time she will totally reform people and structures externally.

The largest African-American cemetery in the mid-South is Zion Cemetery located right in the heart of Memphis. Privately owned by a church denomination that lacks the resources to keep up the grounds, the cemetery is in a state of complete disarray. Most grave markers cannot be seen due to overgrown grass. Abandoned cars are parked there, used as a hideout for local criminals and crackheads. It really is a sight for sore eyes.

Some years ago our church decided to get involved and see if we could clean up the grounds. While serving one day I noticed the tomb of what had to have been a wealthy individual who died in 1900. Elaborately constructed, it stood out from the rest, and not only for its artistic sophistication—a towering oak tree had grown right through the side of the structure. Somehow, an acorn dropped into the ground right along the edge of the tomb, and over the past century it had turned the tomb on its side, totally transforming it.

I don't want you to think that I'm advocating an "each one reach one" theology that seeks to focus on the heart and never addresses the unjust structures of our time. This has been the classic argument of some Christians throughout the years, many of them conveniently not being on the wrong side of the system. A healthy understanding of the gospel forces one to address matters of injustice, no matter how entrenched those systems may be. Christians should be a part of the political process, working with all their might to change these wicked systems. Isn't this the example of England's great abolitionist, William Wilberforce?

Rolling Up Our Sleeves

By no means am I antigovernment. How could I be as a Christian when Romans 13 tells us that government has been established by God (verses 1–7)? Because of this Christians shouldn't dismiss the political process and avoid government, seeing it as bad. Instead we should roll up our sleeves and become involved in the political process. One of the beauties of a democracy is that you and I *can* participate in bringing change. God tells us to "seek the welfare of [our] city" (Jeremiah 29:7).

Can I really say that I'm seeking the welfare of my city or nation when I don't vote? I believe that one of the most caring, Christ-exalting things I can do is to love my city and nation by exercising my legal right to vote.

Voting is just one part of caring for our country through the government. Sure, there are times when we can use the government as an instrument of change by working in tandem with it and voting for candidates who represent our biblical convictions. On other occasions, however, we can use the government to ignite change by standing against it.

In England, William Wilberforce and a host of fellow citizens boycotted sugar and other such staples that were directly connected to the institution of slavery. It was their way of saying to the government that they were vehemently opposed to the injustice the authorities had sanctioned.

I believe that when Christians boycott in love, expressing opposition to the issue and great care and concern for the people, they can become a powerful force for change. After all, didn't we see this with the Civil Rights Movement?

> When Christians boycott in love they can become a powerful force for change.

A cautious word should be given here. Christians have not garnered a favorable reputation for separating issues from people in the political process. What I mean by this is that you can find us with our signs, and at times shouting voices and mean spirits, standing against injustices like abortion, but lost in all of this is a sense of genuine care and concern for the women who are contemplating such a major decision. Whenever our opposition to the issue becomes louder than our concern and love for the people, we've brought dishonor to our Lord.

Where Our Hope Lies

Where we need to repent is when we become more passionate about government than the church of Jesus Christ, the kingdom of God. Government is not the hope of the world; Christ and the community of the beloved, redeemed by the blood of the Lamb are! What are we saying when a so-called follower of Jesus Christ has no hesitations joining a political party but will not join a local church? Is this not a clear declaration of where your hope lies?

If government was the hope of the world, then Christ would have come as a Roman senator, a general, or better yet, part of the line of Caesar.

He most certainly would not have been born to a young teenage girl from a Podunk village called Nazareth, where His first cries were alongside animals in a lowly manger.

Yes, we need to be concerned about our government and the decisions of its leaders. But our hope can never rest in legislation by our representatives. Even Christians will disagree about what is right action. No greater example of that exists than the civil rights legislation of 1965. Christians led the Civil Rights Movement, and the church became the rallying point at a grassroots level for this moral force that would create radically new paradigms for how we live with one another today. Yet the most vocal opponents to the movement were likewise church-attending people, some of whom served on the police forces that unleashed ferocious dogs on peaceful marchers, while others, more militant, served in the KKK. Both sides appealed to the same Scriptures to justify their completely opposite opinions. At issue here is how each side viewed the gospel.

Martin Luther King's famous *Letter from a Birmingham Jail* painfully illustrates the divide among Christians when it came to the gospel in the 1960s. The letter, which became a manifesto of sorts for the movement, was written in response to local clergy, self-professed followers of Jesus Christ, who wanted King to wait and simply let time take its course. Dr. King's understanding of the gospel led him to rail against the social structures of the day. The local clergy, who wanted him to not push so hard, were content with the social norms of the day. Both sides claimed to love and follow Jesus, and because of this the Christian church seemed to have arrived at an impasse. Later a consensus and a sense of moral obligation moved Democrats and Republicans to pass the 1965 Civil Rights Act.

When I see Christians at odds with each other, like in the case of the Civil Rights Movement, I wonder about our focus. Both sides are sincere with their positions. But both can't be right. Rather than argue politics, we need to consult Scripture and ask the Lord to lead us to wisdom. Yet with our fallible minds and selfish hearts, we will not always see clearly or make the right decisions. As we pursue justice and righteousness through our local and federal governments, we need to recognize that politics will not have lasting answers that ensure fair and wise laws.

As it stands, the real political question in America is not one of donkeys or elephants, Democrats or Republicans. Neither party can contain the fullness of the kingdom of God. Instead, the issue is one of a democracy versus a theocracy, a government run by human beings or one ruled by God. Humans have no power outside of what an omnipotent, all-powerful God measures out to them. We can continue to argue and divide over impotent governments, or we can place our hope in an all-powerful God whose theocracy is the bride of Christ.

4 THE GOSPEL AND O. J. SIMPSON

To be anti-racist is not to be colorblind but color-
embracing—even lovestruck with each other![1]

Cornel West

My grandfather could tell you exactly where he was when news reached him that the Japanese had bombed Pearl Harbor. Both of my parents can still recall in vivid detail where they were when they received the tragic news that President Kennedy was assassinated, and a few years later when Dr. Martin Luther King Jr. was slain. In the same way, I can describe with pinpoint clarity where I was and what I was doing on the morning of September 11, 2001, when the World Trade Center towers collapsed. Every generation has its defining moments, when a monumental tragedy unites the people in unspeakable grief.

October 3, 1995, was another historical marker for my generation. If the date doesn't ring a bell, let me remind you: this was the day that the O. J. Simpson murder trial verdict was delivered. I don't have the greatest of memories (my wife likes to say I have "convenient amnesia"—I can memorize a sermon but "forget" to take out the trash), but I still remember everything about that day. I was working at a large black church in Atlanta, trying to save some money for seminary while gaining ministry experience. The church had somewhat of a corporate feel to it, where

> For us, the verdict that day wasn't about O. J.; it was about being black in America.

everyone's time was meticulously accounted for. So it was a little surprising that on this day we were allowed to leave our desks to go to the conference room for an extended period of time to watch the verdict.

The buildup to the verdict was as exciting and intense as watching the pregame festivities of the NCAA national championship game when your favorite team is playing. For me and my African-American friends gathered in the conference room that day, O. J. was on *our* team. Now don't get me wrong; prior to all this mess, none of us cared about O. J. Simpson. None of my friends went out of their way to buy Isotoner gloves or rent from Hertz because these were products he endorsed. In fact, we shook our heads at O. J. for simply being another rich black man who, once he made it, gave the impression that he forgot about his people and married a white woman. I hope you sincerely forgive my spiritual immaturity, but I'm just telling you that this is how we felt at the time.

On October 3, the jury found Simpson innocent of charges that he had murdered his former wife and her acquaintance. For us, the verdict that day wasn't about O. J.; it was about being black in America, and when he was declared not guilty, my friends and I shamefully high-fived each other and celebrated. Even though we knew in the pit of our souls that O. J. did it, we didn't care. We danced and hollered like we had just won the lottery, because it felt like *we* had finally won. Our minds rolled back to the cases involving Emmett Till, Medgar Evers, and hundreds of other court cases where beyond the shadow of a doubt it was clear that the white men on trial had committed the heinous acts of murder, but they were let off. Finally, finally, on this October day the tables were turned because we had gotten one over, just as *they* had.

Our joy in the days to come only grew when we saw the looks of devastating sadness that seemed to capture every white person. *Finally*, we thought, *they know how we felt for decades, if not centuries, being on the wrong side of the system.* I still remember one of my black friends smiling in exultation as the camera panned to several tearful white ladies who were obviously incensed at the injustice. My friend didn't deny the injustice (none of us did); he just yelled at the television, "Now you're upset? Where was this same conviction just a few years ago with Rodney King?"[2]

It shames me to write these words. Over the past fifteen years I've matured a lot, and God has done a work of grace in my life. My mind-set and actions during the O. J. Simpson murder trial revealed a racist heart and an ugly dimension of my life that causes me to cringe today. God's work in my heart has been so drastic that the before and after shot is laughable—I'm now that guy who married outside of my culture, something I never thought I'd do; and instead of working at a black church, I'm helping to lead a majority white church. While there still remains a residue of racism in my heart, I'm walking the road of repentance. I'm a recovering racist.

Prior to the Simpson trial, I never thought I was a racist. My parents worked for a majority white nonprofit Christian organization, and because of this I spent a lot of time with white people, even establishing some meaningful friendships. When the verdict came down in 1995, I had just graduated from a majority white Bible college,

> O. J. Simpson taught us a truth that most of us are uncomfortable admitting: race is a bigger issue than we'd like to think.

and even though I had experienced some racism there, I thought I had weathered the storm well and would have considered myself to be an emotionally healthy person who loved everyone. After all, some of my best friends were white!

But for some unexplainable reason, a former college and NFL All-Pro running back accused of murdering his white ex-wife and her friend exposed me, along with thousands (if not millions) of other blacks and whites across our nation. Like a kitchen light suddenly coming on, the insects of racism that we had tried to confine in our souls were exposed for the world to see. O. J. Simpson taught us a truth that most of us are uncomfortable admitting: race is a bigger issue than we'd like to think.

I want to explore both the issue of racism and diversity in light of the gospel. In this chapter we're going to discover that diversity is a beautiful thing, but when we pursue it apart from the cross of Christ, we are guilty of idolatry. Finally, we'll end by walking through Revelation 5:9–10 where we'll see the connection between the gospel and diversity, and how we can practically experience gospel-driven diversity in our relationships and churches.

Decades Ago, Right?

You maybe wondering if race is still an issue today, and your question is completely legitimate. Since the O. J. Simpson murder trial, we've seen the rise of postmodern culture and its value of tolerance. One of the beautiful things about tolerance is its sense of inclusiveness, and racial equality and harmony. Without exception, all of my white friends apologize repeatedly for the racism of their parents and previous generations. Many of them are leading the fight for more diverse churches. In fact, I continue to meet with church leaders and business owners who seem genuinely sincere about wanting to hire qualified minorities to promote diversity. We even have an African-American president. So what's the big deal? Racism has got to be extinct, right?

Not so fast. Every minority person I know has a current racism story to tell, including me. I was visiting a church the first Sunday of our vacation, there to hear God's Word and worship Him with my family. Sometime earlier I had been invited to be a guest teacher but declined because of my own responsibilities at Fellowship Memphis. Now, during the serving of Communion, I was reflecting about Christ's sacrifice for me. In the middle of my meditation a white man, who was a leader at the church and who had tried for a period of time to get me to teach at the church, noticed me. He marched over to me and threatened to kick a certain "black" part of my anatomy because I had the "audacity" to attend his church while at the same time being unable to teach for him. Needless to say, I was stunned. The year was 2010, fifteen years after the Simpson verdict.

> The comments on my Facebook page revealed that whites and minorities still remain worlds apart when it comes to the race issue.

Even more curious were the reactions I received when I posted this incident on my Facebook page (I obviously kept his name and the name of the church anonymous). All of my minority friends who responded either shared a current story of racism or vividly described what they would have done, and it didn't involve turning the other cheek. Most of my white friends questioned my decision to share this with the world. Why stir things up? In their minds, this was an isolated incident from a person who didn't represent the norm, so why even bring attention to it?

The comments on my Facebook page revealed that whites and minorities still remain worlds apart when it comes to the race issue. In my experience, many minorities want to talk about issues of race, while many of our white brothers and sisters want to simply move on. But without any real meaningful dialogue, authentic diverse community is at a standstill.

In Tyler Perry's movie *Why Did I Get Married?*, we are introduced to a couple who have experienced an unspeakable tragedy. Due to an oversight on the mother's part, she forgot to strap her two-year-old son in his car seat. Moments later they get into a car accident and he dies. She naturally blames herself, and the husband wrestles with anger toward his bride. What makes matters worse, though, is that every time he wants to talk about the tragedy she shuts down, refusing to engage. To the wife it's merely something that happened in the past, and they just need to move on. The husband can't move on unless they talk. She refuses. So for the next several years this couple is living together, but not experiencing any intimacy. Ultimately the marriage ends in a bitter divorce, not because the child died but because they refused to do the hard thing and talk about the incident.

Similarly those in the body of Christ who have not experienced racism personally often wonder, "Why can't we just move past this?" But as followers of Jesus Christ, all of us are placed into a network of relationships with many people who have been affected by racism. Can you and I really say we love our ethnically different brothers and sisters and have an authentic relationship with them, but choose to ignore a major part of who they are?

The Problem with Diversity

When we arrived in Memphis to plant our church, we came wanting to experience a Revelation 5:9–10 community, where people from "every tribe and language and people and nation" would come and worship and do life together. That is the picture—the reality—of life in heaven.

By God's grace we are seeing this happen in a city where no one ever thought it could, in part because we've not shied away from the hard discussions on race. Because of this, word has gotten out that Fellowship Memphis is that "racially diverse church." While I see the people's point, I'm uncomfortable with this label, because it suggests that racial diversity is the primary thing that we're after, and it's not.

The heartbeat of our church is the gospel of Jesus Christ. We labor really hard through our preaching and ministry programs to reinforce this truth. This is of life-and-death importance to me, because if anything replaces the centrality of the gospel and the cross of Jesus Christ, I've just constructed an idol; and one of the biggest idols I'm seeing churches in a postmodern culture erect is the idol of diversity.

Yes, I'm excited to see both church plants and existing churches express a sincere desire to become more racially inclusive and diverse. As I consult with pastors across the country, I see sincere hearts who are willing to do whatever it takes to get there, even if it means going to war with a racist constituency in their church. Where I tend to get a little nervous, though, is when diversity and not the gospel becomes the epicenter; then we're in danger of the sin of idolatry and turning diversity into a church growth technique.

It's not just churches who are celebrating diversity, but people in general are expressing more than a passing interest in establishing an inclusive community of friendships. Both my Christian and non-Christian friends revel in the diversity of their relationships. But while these relationships are unprecedented in American history (at least to this scale), postmodern culture's emphasis on relativism has limited the depth these inclusive communities can plumb. After all, if what's true for you is only true for you, who are you then to challenge my lifestyle choices or any other decisions I embrace? And if the "community" I traffic in is handcuffed from challenging me, how can there be genuine growth? What really tethers and binds these relationships together?

Authentic Gospel and Diversity

Biblical community has always celebrated diversity, but because of the centrality of the gospel, diversity does not become a rallying cry; Jesus does. What this means is that Christ-followers have a reference point, a north star, if you will, to challenge and encourage one another, to genuinely love one another and experience what the writers of the New Testament called *fellowship*. My race never becomes the focal point in

> Racial diversity is not an essential for salvation; the gospel of Jesus Christ is.

Christocentric community; Jesus does.

Our conversations on race and our attempts to bring people together should not be divorced from the cross, because when this happens we turn into mere sociologists, diminishing the power of the crucified Christ. Racial diversity is not an essential for salvation; the gospel of Jesus Christ is. However, where the gospel is truly and authentically preached and lived, we should expect to see diversity. This should be a natural fruit of the gospel, part of that horizontal axis of the cross that reaches into lives in the Christian community as well as the lives of the spiritually lost.

With that, here are suggestions on how we can contribute to racial justice in four areas: *racial diversity*, *a celebration of God and diversity*, *intentionality*, and *making sacrifices*.

"All People Groups"

We can contribute through welcoming diversity in the churches. An example of this is Redeemer Presbyterian Church in New York City, led by senior pastor Tim Keller. Listen to Pastor Keller's messages and you won't hear a barrage of sermons on race. Instead what you'll hear in every sermon is the gospel. The gospel, though, offers reconciliation. Not unexpectedly, the fruit of Tim's gospel preaching is a church filled with racial diversity.

So many passages connect the gospel with diversity. In John 3:16 we see God's incredible love for the world—hear "all people groups"—inspiring Him to send His only Son, Jesus, to die for our sins that we might have eternal life. Revisiting Jesus' conversation with the Samaritan woman in John 4, we see the proclamation of the gospel yielding the fruit of an ethnically different people group being received into the kingdom. Peter's proclamation of the gospel on the Day of Pentecost resulted in the first converts being a multiethnic community of faith (Acts 2:5–11). These are but a few examples in the Scriptures that show us that where the gospel is first preached and proclaimed as central, the fruit is racial diversity. By far, the most powerful racial diversity strategy a church can ever hope to have is the clear preaching of the gospel of Jesus Christ.

> Once I truly understood that forgiveness is the essence of the gospel I was constrained to forgive.

The same is true for the individuals who come to church. One of the ways we really know that the gospel has taken root in the heart of a person is that they gravitate toward diversity. Genuinely redeemed people engage the poor (Matthew 25), cross racial lines (Acts 10), and any other sinful barrier because they understand that the gospel is for all people.

People will often come up to me at Fellowship Memphis to tell me they're moving. Usually, they'll ask me at some point to recommend a church that's just like ours in the city where they're relocating. It's not uncommon to hear them say something to the effect of, "Because I just can't go back to an all-black, or an all-white church." The gospel has changed the way they view community and church.

The gospel is a balm of healing. One major reason I acted in such a prejudiced way during the O. J. Simpson trial is because just two years before a white classmate of mine in Bible college had called me the "n-word." His words wounded me deeply, and because I refused to forgive, a seed of bitterness took root that took me years to recover. My pathway to recovery came via the gospel. Once I truly understood that forgiveness is the essence of the gospel—that just like this man who shamed and violated me, I had done the exact same thing to God, yet He in His infinite grace and mercy has forgiven me—I was constrained by the gospel to forgive.

But that's not all. As my anger subsided and I allowed the Holy Spirit to do in and through me what I could never do in my own strength—forgive this brother—I discovered that a passion was growing in me to be a vessel of both vertical and horizontal reconciliation. I wanted others to experience the joy of seeing former enemies being reconciled to one another through the gospel of Jesus Christ. Fifteen years ago, while I was high-fiving my buddies over the O. J. verdict, if you would have said to me that I would marry a woman half-white and half-Mexican, lead a multicultural church, and be passionate about seeing the races come together, I would have laughed. What is transforming my life is not being around some cool white people who get it, but the gospel. Because of this, when that church leader threatened to kick a "black" part of my body, I was able to tell him that I forgave him. How could I not? The gospel compels me to forgive and be reconciled to my brother.

When the gospel has taken root in a person's life, or in the life of their church, a desire for all peoples will be evident. Although there are natural exceptions to this, especially if you live in a place where there is no racial diversity, by and large we can expect racial diversity when we live and proclaim a biblical gospel. That's why in John's vision of the church united in heaven, he sees a multiethnic, multicultural throng of "people for God from every tribe and language and people and nation" (Revelation 5:9).

What John Saw

In this vision of heaven and the end times recorded in Revelation, God pulls back the curtain of heaven and allows John a sneak peak at what is taking place, including the nations worshiping God together.

In fact, the worship of God is the central event of heaven. For all of eternity we will be worshiping Him. But John doesn't stop with God, the One being worshiped; he is careful to point out the kind of worshipers who are there—people from "every tribe and language." The worshipers are ethnically diverse. How did this diverse community of worshipers get to heaven? John writes that they were "ransomed" by the blood of Jesus (verse 9).

Notice, they're not celebrating diversity. They're celebrating God!

As we walk through Revelation 5:9–10, God is going to show John three critical truths about racial or ethnic diversity. These three things are vital if we're going to be agents of healing and horizontal reconciliation, especially in a nation that has been scarred deeply by racism. The first is a *celebration of God*.

John watched as these worshipers "sang a new song." The Greek word for song means "to wail." In fact, this word was used of a woman in childbirth, and the loud sounds she would make especially in a pre-epidural world! The singing here is not some passive, quiet mumbling of words. No, this is loud, top-of-the-voice kind of singing. But what are they celebrating?

The apostle John goes on: "And they sang a new song, saying, 'Worthy are you to take the scroll.'" Notice, they're not celebrating diversity. They're celebrating God! The focus of heaven is not on the worshipers and their ethnic differences, but the focus of heaven is on the One being worshiped—God!

When native Memphians come to our church for the first time and see a diverse body of believers, they will often make a beeline to me, give me a hug, and say something to the effect that they never thought this could happen. They're amazed by the diversity, and they vow to come back. I'm grateful to God for this, and if He so chooses to use diversity as a means to do a work of grace in people's lives through the gospel, then praise God! But diversity doesn't get anyone into heaven; only God and the gospel does.

Revelation 5:9–10 teaches us that God and His glorious gospel must always be the center of our celebration, not diversity. But our passage also allows us to celebrate that diversity.

One frequently asked question about heaven is, "Will we be able to recognize one another when we're there?" While the focus of heaven will be on the Creator and not the reunion with our dearly beloved spouse, family members, or friends, I do believe that we will be able to recognize each other in heaven. There are two biblical evidences for this. First is looking at Jesus' postresurrection, glorified body. While He was no longer contained by things such as walls or doors but could just walk through them, appearing in a room, His new glorified body retained some definite physical characteristics. He could be touched, the wounds were still there, and He could be recognized. Second, how does John, looking into heaven, notice that there were people from every nation, tribe, and language? I think the answer to this is that John *saw* color; he *saw* ethnic differences.

This is important for us, because God is not color-blind. People tend to say that they don't see color, and while I get the gist of what they're saying—that they don't allow someone's ethnic differences to inspire prejudice in them—the statement is both personally offensive, and biblically incorrect. Psalm 139:14 tells me that "I am fearfully and wonderfully made." God, in great artistic detail, made me who I am. My personality, stature, physical appearance, passions, likes and dislikes all bear His image. Ephesians 2:10 tells me that I am His masterpiece. A part of what this means is that my color, especially seen across the tapestry of humanity, brings Him great joy and delight, so much so, that when I die and receive my new glorified body, that my blackness or someone's yellowness or whiteness or brownness will still be intact. God the artist would have been bored to death looking at one color, so He created many colors. This is to be celebrated, not ignored. Moving from color blindness to celebration when it comes to diversity will position us to experience gospel-driven, God glorifying diversity. Scholar Cornel West writes, "To be anti-racist is not to be color-blind but color-embracing, even lovestruck with each other!"

So let's celebrate diversity. Yet a caution about such celebration: let's not become so passionate about it that our affections for our culture exceed our affections for Christ. Paul understood this well; that's why he would tell the Galatians that in Christ "there is neither Jew nor Greek" (3:28). Again, he's not denying racial differences, but what he is saying is that now that the believer's identity is in the cross, all other affections become secondary.

Tony Evans says that it's grammatically and theologically incorrect to say that someone is a "Black Christian," because when they say this they put "Christian" in the noun position and "Black" in the adjective position. The rules of English dictate that adjectives modify nouns, and nothing, Dr. Evans says, is to modify one's Christianity but Christ and Christ alone.

How do people know if they've crossed the line and celebrated their culture or diversity to the point of idolatry? I think the answer to this can be found in what causes us the deepest pain or ignites anger. For me, race at times was an idol. I can recall some of my most depressing days and shameful outbursts have centered around the issue of race. In fact, my strongest battles with releasing bitterness and extending forgiveness have been directly tied to me being culturally and racially offended. Yes, we should all be incensed at injustice, but I do believe that there's a direct correlation between personal idols and our most intense hurts.

Being Intentional

Revelation 5:9–10 also shows us the key element of intentionality when it comes to diversity. John sees a wonderful mixture of people from every ethnic group worshiping God, but how did this happen? "For you were slain, and by your blood you *ransomed* people for God from every tribe and language and people and nation" (verse 9, emphasis added). Diversity exists in heaven because of the intentionality of Jesus Christ. The Greek word for "ransomed" comes from a root word that is commonly translated as marketplace. John pictures Christ going to the marketplace of humanity and specifically choosing people from every ethnicity. The diversity in heaven does not happen by accident but stems from the sovereign choosing of the crucified, now resurrected Christ.

How can churches become racially diverse? Taking our cues from our passage in Revelation, it's clear such change does not happen by accident but by being intentional.

At our church we have a preaching team that rotates throughout our various locations. Two of the teachers are white, and the other two are African American. Our worship department is diverse with a worship leader being Columbian, and the other African American. Our elder team is racially diverse, with about 60 percent of the team being white, and the rest being African American. Is it any wonder that our church is racially diverse? We've taken prayerful intentional steps to become racially diverse.

Jesus models this principle of intentionality not just in His postresurrection ministry, but we see it in His earthly ministry. At a time when Jews never would have gone directly through Samaria, even though it would have made the journey quicker, Jesus breaks with the cultural norms and intentionally stops there to spark a revival. He was intentional.

My heart is overwhelmed with joy as I think of many people in the kingdom who have followed Jesus' example of intentionality when it comes to diversity. I know of several white families in our church who could be living in more comfortable communities, but have instead chosen to be the minority by moving into African-American impoverished places, not to save them but to be with them and to love them. This has to bring joy to our heavenly Father. Other members, because we don't do a Vacation Bible School program, intentionally go to churches that are ethnically different from what they're used to in order to meet parents in the hopes of forming relationships. This is but another purposeful step to experience what John saw in heaven here on earth. If my life is not experiencing a Revelation 5:9–10 community, could it be that I have not gone the way of intentionality?

Making a Sacrifice

Diversity isn't cheap; it comes with an expensive price tag. At the end of verse 9 we see the costliness of diversity: "for you were *slain*, and *by your blood* you ransomed people for God from every tribe and language and people and nation" (italics mine). We've already noticed that the diversity we'll experience in heaven comes about through the intentional, sovereign selection of Jesus Christ, but this diversity also comes through the blood of Jesus. If it wasn't for the sacrifice of Christ, there would be no diversity.

Nothing of long-term meaning ever happens apart from sacrifice. This is especially true when it comes to racial diversity and ethnic inclusion. At our church we experience this every Sunday with the music. Our worship leaders are skilled at taking a song that may be familiar to our white brothers and sisters and add a dash of soul to it so that our African-American attenders can relate. They can also take gospel songs and ease up on them a bit for our white attenders. But you know what? At the end of the set no one ever says that they sang every song they liked the way that they liked it, and we're okay with that. What we've come to experience is that to fight for racial diversity at the same time means that we have to go to war with the American god of comfort. Could it be that the reason so many churches express a desire to be ethnically diverse but fail to experience it is because they are unwilling to challenge people to sacrifice and give up their preferences?

> To fight for racial diversity, we have to go to war with the American god of comfort.

Watch a game of baseball, particularly a close game, and you'll often see a batter bunt the ball. This simply involves placing both hands on the bat and making contact so that the ball rolls slowly down the first or third base lines. Now, no batter dreams of bunting. He'd love to swing for the fences, so when he gets the signal from the third base coach, he's probably not thrilled. But these batters bunt anyway. Why? So that they can advance the runner into scoring position, thus giving their team a chance to win. See, bunting demands sacrificing my own rights and desires for the good of the team. It means thinking of others instead of thinking of myself.[3]

If we're going to realize diversity in our churches and relationships, we have to become good "bunters." We have to be willing to sacrifice personal preferences and rights for the good of others. What exactly does this look like for you personally? Maybe it's putting your kid in an athletic league that's ethnically different from what he's used to so that you can sacrificially and intentionally form relationships with kids and parents who don't look like you. Or maybe it's prayerfully pursuing a friendship with someone, being vulnerable enough to ask questions in an attempt to get to know them. It could be joining a church that's literally on the other side of the tracks.

The Gospel and Race

In offering these four action steps, I'm aware some will still argue that the Bible doesn't talk about race the way that we do. Some claim that the Bible knows of only two races of people: the human race and the new race made up of all those ethnicities who have embraced Jesus Christ as Lord and Savior. I don't want to engage in the details of this argument, because I think we can tend to forget that words primarily have meaning in relationship to other words and current contexts. Words evolve over time, and to an American living in the twenty-first century the term *race* is used interchangeably by most with *ethnicity*, so this is how I will use the word *race* or *racism*.

Even though there may be a difference of opinion over what exactly the Bible means when it comes to race, it is safe to conclude that the Bible doesn't shy away from what we would today call racism. When Miriam and Aaron, the siblings of Moses, had a problem with Moses' wife, Zipporah, because of her ethnicity, God called a meeting and judged their racist actions (Numbers 12:1–4). Centuries later when King Solomon entered into a flurry of interracial relationships, God made it clear that His problem with Solomon's choice of women was not on the grounds of racial differences but spiritual differences (1 Kings 11:2).

Later on in the New Testament, we see Jesus violating racial and gender taboos by conversing with a Samaritan woman in broad daylight, helping to bring the presence of the kingdom to a group of people ethnically different than He (John 4:4–9). When Peter discriminates against the Gentiles because of their race, Paul, a fellow Jew, calls Peter out on his racism and says that he is acting out of step with the gospel (Galatians 2:11–15).

These are just a few examples of many instances in the Bible where God and His people are willing to violate racial norms and have difficult conversations in order to spread God's purposes here on earth. God and His people in the Scriptures model to us a willingness to talk about race.

As members of Christ's glorious church, let's deal with racial inequities in our communities by welcoming diversity, celebrating God and His diverse worshipers, being intentional, and sacrificing our comfort. Indeed, all four steps entail our willingness to give up comfort. Are you willing to do this? I sure hope so.

5 THE OTHER SIDE OF THE TRACKS

The strong must disadvantage themselves for the weak, the majority for the minority, or the community frays and the fabric breaks.[1]

Tim Keller

Some years ago I was wrapping up an interview with a church elder. He had been a member of this particular church for decades. He had seen the best and the worst days. I finally asked him what he loved most about his church and the pastor. Without hesitating, he said, "You know, prior to our current pastor coming here, when I would come to church on Sunday, it would be nothing for me to be in a line behind six Mercedes trying to find a decent parking spot. Now when I come to church I'm behind a lot of pickup trucks with a few Mercedes sprinkled in."

I got his point—the church had gone through an extreme makeover so that what was once a strictly middle- to upper-middle-class church now had become an economically diverse church where the rich worshiped alongside the not-so-rich.

I found his words to be inspiring and deflating all at once. I was moved by the transformation that was taking place in this wonderful church. But at the same time, the gleam in his eyes at what God was doing was an indicator light that this was abnormal for the church of Jesus Christ. After all, who brags about normal, right?

When we go back to day one of the church, however, we realize that diversity, and especially socioeconomic diversity, *were* normal. Luke reports, "And all who believed were together and had all things in common. And they were selling their possessions and belongings and distributing the proceeds to all, as any had need" (Acts 2:44–45).

The first church was made up of those who were wealthy and those who were poor. We know that there were those who had means because some were able to sell their possessions. In other words, there were people in the church who had it to give. Maybe it was a second home in the hills or at the lake they were able to unload. Or maybe it was that late-model chariot with twenty-four-inch rims that they simply gave to those who had no means of transportation. There were people who had means in the church.

> God has incredible compassion for the poor and the marginalized of society.

But as the writer of Acts, Luke makes it very clear that most in the church didn't have the second home or the fancy ride. Some were probably without any home or transportation at all. This is why the possessions were being sold and given to these people. The picture Luke is painting for us is a pretty drastic one. In fact, in all probability the Sunday morning parking lot would have late-model chariots and people who *walked*! And to think that this is how the church *began*. This was the church's *normal*!

In this chapter we are going to ask the question, "If the gospel is about establishing radically new paradigms in relationships and how I view the world and people, how does this impact my thinking and actions in regard to class?" We're going to see that the Scriptures, from beginning to end, reveal a God who thinks highly of and has incredible compassion for the poor and the marginalized of society. From here we'll explore how we can practically prepare ourselves to engage the marginalized of society by going to war with the American god of greed and materialism. Finally, we'll end with some practical steps on how to build an economically diverse community.

We know that as churches appeared across the Roman Empire, socioeconomic diversity became the norm within those churches, because the topic kept coming up in Paul's letters. Without fail, Paul deals with the theme of relationships in all of his letters. He is concerned that these new Christ-followers learn how to get along with one another. Relationships can be messy in general, but especially when you deal with fundamental differences such as class. And in just about every single letter that Paul writes, the issue of class differences comes up.

Breaking Down the Walls

To the Ephesians and the Colossians, he gives instructions on how slaves and their masters need to relate with one another, the implication being that both groups attended the same church (Ephesians 6:5–9; Colossians 3:18–4:1). In fact the book of Philemon is expressly written to help a slave owner navigate the relationship with his fugitive, recently turned follower of Jesus, Onesimus. And while we correctly think of the issue of men and women in the early church as relating to gender, we would also do well to remember that there are strong undertones of class involved because women were seen as inferior to men, in some sense as nothing more than a piece of property.

In Roman culture, a firm class structure was in place that established social fences limiting how people related to one another. There was no such thing as aristocracy sharing a meal or doing life with the poor. Women could not even think about becoming a Roman senator, much less a witness in court. In fact, Rome's class structure was so entrenched that the residue of it began to be felt among the Jews, who looked at the mealtimes as opportunities to solidify one's place in society. Because of this they were appalled at Jesus, a man who claimed to be the Messiah, who would dare eat with tax collectors and allow His meals to be interrupted by lowly prostitutes. There were both a moral and a class issue involved. Yet the glorious beauty of Jesus and the early church was its absolute defiance of the class norms of its day. Pulsating with the gospel, both sought to create new norms where in Christ there is neither "slave nor free." And it was this new norm that made the church so attractive.

Living in Memphis I became well acquainted with the story of the Academy Award–winning *The Blind Side* long before it became a movie. Several years ago a member of our church put a copy of Michael Lewis's book (called by the same title as the movie) in my hands. I have to confess that I almost didn't make it past the first third of the book. The story was all too familiar, and seemed all too repulsive at the same time: poor kid from the hood with no education whose daddy was nowhere to be found has worlds of talent and gets rescued by the wealthy heroes. *Thanks, but I've seen this way too many times before*, I thought.

But I felt compelled to continue. I seemed to be catching glimpses of authentic love from this affluent family. A couple of times my eyes moistened and tears ran down my face as I saw them embrace this young man, inviting him into their home, and treating him as they actually saw him— as their son. Here this man brought nothing to the table by way of material goods. He was a hopeless young man from the worst part of the city. Yet the Tuohy family gave him more than a chance; they gave him what his soul longed for—love. He became part of their family. It is this moving picture of authentic love between the wealthy and the poor that resonated so deeply with a world whose "normal" is class division. And I think it was because of this that audiences flocked to the theaters, and it won actress Sandra Bullock an Academy Award.

That lack of class distinction helped the early church grow and flourish. It had become the only place in Roman society where a guest could stand at the doorway and see the rich washing the feet of the poor. Here women also were esteemed and found value within a larger society that saw them as little more than objects.

Taking one's seat during the meeting, the guest would open his eyes in shock at the sight of a man whom he knew to be a slave sitting with his master. The way they related to one another was not typical. There seemed to be a genuine fondness and love for one another.

The power of the gospel unleashed before this guest's eyes was like watching the walls of class came tumbling down.

Two Thousand Verses!

To be sure, God's heart for His covenant people to embrace the poor did not emerge in the New Testament when His church was birthed. No, this was a dream that God spoke centuries before. In fact, the Bible contains verse after verse articulating God's heart for the poor, the widowed, the orphan, and the disenfranchised. Some have actually counted over two thousand verses in the Bible where God speaks of His heart for the less fortunate; and many of these passages are instructions for His covenant people to engage them. Here are a few:

But there will be no poor among you. (Deuteronomy 15:4)

If among you, one of your brothers should become poor, in any of your towns within your land that the Lord your God is giving you, you shall not harden your heart or shut your hand against your poor brother, but you shall open your hand to him and lend him sufficient for his need, whatever it may be. (Deuteronomy 15:7–8)

When you reap the harvest of your land, you shall not reap your field right up to its edge, neither shall you gather the gleanings after your harvest. And you shall not strip your vineyard bare, neither shall you gather the fallen grapes of your vineyard. You shall leave them for the poor and for the sojourner: I am the Lord your God. (Leviticus19:9–10)

A Little Extra on the Side

In the Leviticus passage God is establishing His welfare system for Israel—and please notice that it is not a system of enablement but empowerment. God is clear: if the poor want to eat, let them come and work! We see this modeled in the book of Ruth. When Ruth encounters a bad season in her life and is in need of quick relief, she obeys this command of God and goes to work as a poor person in the field of a man named Boaz.

Now, I do not think that our welfare system should be totally abolished. There are some people who desperately need welfare . . . for a season. My mother, in fact, was on welfare for a time during her life. But I do agree with those who say that our welfare system has become the new slave master for many in our culture because of its failure to empower by promoting long-term employment. In contrast, when God set up the economic system for Israel, He did so understanding that some would be poor, and the poor were not to be sent to some impersonal governmental office. Instead, each individual was to display compassion and act responsibly, helping those without for a season by giving out of their own resources.

God is clear as well in speaking to the person with means. This person was to not selfishly consume or sell all of their produce. Instead the rich were to intentionally and generously leave margin in their fields for the poor to come and glean. Boaz obeys this command, and his reward was a wife. Maybe God is saying to the single brothers out there to leave margin in your budgets and you'll get a woman! I'm just saying.

While there's a bit of humor in that last remark, what is not so funny is God's command to leave "margin." Here I think is where we can take the principle that God instructs an agricultural community and apply it to a more urban setting like ours. I believe the nugget of timeless truth we mine out from here is that God expects His people to leave "margins"— a little extra on the side—in their budget to spontaneously and generously care for the poor. That when we come to our budgets, we don't max them out on savings and shopping and houses and other stuff. But we leave room to bless the poor. How much room or margin should we leave? God doesn't say. He never tells the people of Israel how much margin to leave in their fields. I think the reason God is so ambiguous is because if generosity is legislated, it fails to be generous.

The Question of Enough

What leaving margin really comes down to is the question of enough. Every follower of Jesus Christ must learn to ask the question, "How much is enough?" Specifically, How much is enough house? How much is enough income? How much is enough clothes? How much is enough purses, shoes—savings even? These questions run counter to the society in which we live. Materialism is so entrenched in America that trying to explain it is like trying to explain water to a fish! It's just the culture we live in. Some have estimated that by the time a person turns twenty they would have seen over one million commercials! The essence of commercials is you don't have enough—buy our product!

As a college student at Oxford, John Wesley asked the question of enough. He looked at the coming year and wanted to set a line for how much he needed to live on for that year. He concluded twenty-eight pounds for that year was enough. Anything he made over that, he would simply give away. That year he actually made thirty pounds. He lived off the twenty-eight and gave the other two away. Wesley felt great about that, so much so that he said he'd stick to that for the rest of his life. Anything John made over twenty-eight pounds, he would simply give away. If you know anything about John Wesley, the

> Enough is freeing. Enough is pure joy!

founder of the Methodist church, a lot of money came his way, especially through his writings. But twenty-eight pounds it was, and twenty-eight pounds it would be. Wesley had settled the enough question.

By American standards my wife, Korie, and I are nowhere near wealthy (although by global standards, we along with just about every other American are). We definitely know what it's like to pinch pennies, especially when you plant a church with twenty-six people in a living room. But now that our church and speaking opportunities have grown substantially, so has our income. To invite you into the private corners of our marriage, I told Korie that I'm *really* scared at the amount of money that's passing through our hands.

In fact, most Americans should be scared. As Randy Alcorn has pointed out, if you only make twenty-five thousand dollars a year with no raises or increases or bonuses for the next forty years, one million dollars will have passed through your hands.[2] That's a lot to give an answer to God for! So I want to invite you to pray about what Korie and I have been praying about, and what we recently said—enough.

We've dreamed as a family of what it would look like to cap our salary and to continue taking the increases but say anything we get over the "enough line," we're giving away (in addition to the 10 percent that God requires). Talk about joy! Do you know the absolute joy that comes when a member of your church calls in desperation saying they made a really bad financial decision and need some immediate relief, and we can provide that for them? Or the joy that I had recently when the Holy Spirit impressed upon me not to take a check for preaching to a really large church, and the look on my host's face when I said thanks but no thanks? Enough is freeing. Enough is pure joy!

Before I move on, I warn both you and me not to get self-righteous here. Ambiguity can be a really hard thing. After all, God didn't legislate the exact dimensions of margin that had to be marked off in the Israelites fields; I'm sure that led to some pretty interesting conversations. Can you see farmer Joe looking at the other guys' fields and wondering why the guy in the field to his right had left so much margin? *Man, who's he trying to impress?* Meanwhile, Joe notices that the guy with the field on his left has set aside a smaller margin than Joe has. Now Joe feels self-righteous because of his own superior margin.

If enough for you is living in a fifteen-hundred-square-foot house, and compared to the other guy at church, that's the size of his guest house, be careful not to be critical. Conversely, if you are able to live in a larger house, don't think too highly of yourself. If enough for you is sticking to used cars, be careful to not look down at the brother who pulls up with the brand-new luxury car. We've got to be really careful to not speak specifically into things that Scripture is unclear about.

On the other hand, I do think most American Christians have missed it profoundly in the area of greed. As Tim Keller pointed out in his book *Counterfeit Gods*, Jesus' command to be watchful of greed is a peculiar one. He doesn't tell us to be watchful of adultery or lying or any other sin. Why? Because we know when we've crossed the line. Greed is not as clear-cut. It's extremely subtle and dangerous, and if we're going to be really honest, most of us don't realize we've crossed the line until we're miles beyond it! A big reason for this is that our standard has become the culture we live in. And when you live in a materialistic and greedy culture, you can justify a lot of things.

Add to this the default of silence when it comes to money and material possessions. It's just taboo for people to talk about what's in their bank accounts, and how they spend their money. Because people are silent about money and how they steward it, churches tend to be silent about it as well.

I've grown up in the church, and I've seen people get called out on a lot of things. I've seen people confronted on their gossip. I've witnessed a couple being confronted for their immorality. But I've never, and I mean never, seen or heard of a case of church discipline where an individual is being confronted on their greed. "Church, today we bring before you sister Johnson. For the past year we've been confronting her on her

> It's just taboo for people to talk about what's in their bank accounts, and how they spend their money.

materialistic ways, and she just hasn't responded." I've never heard of such a thing, have you?

No one has ever said to me, "Pastor, I just had a great conversation with a young man who spent three hundred bucks on a pair of jeans. I pretty much asked him, How can you justify that with world hunger and all the needs it presents?" No one that I know of has ever gone up to a young woman and said, "You know, I've noticed that you're always wearing the latest fashions. Now don't get me wrong. It's okay to want to look nice and feel beautiful, but you strike me as one who seems to care a little bit too much about earthly treasure. Can we talk some about this?"

What's become abnormally normal is to press mute on these questions; to just say "That's their business." This is problematic, because when we walk through the Scriptures we see that God speaks loudly on the issue of money and possessions. There are more than 2,350 verses that capture God's convictions on money and possessions.[3] Jesus spoke loudly on the matter as well. In fact there are more verses in the Bible devoted to money and possessions than to faith and prayer! We must be very careful to root out the lie that money is private and we should keep silent about it. It's just like Satan to want to press mute on what God blasts the volume on.

Saving or Hoarding?

The gospel is invasive, poking its head into every corner of our lives, even our money. In the Sermon on the Mount, Jesus takes time to speak about the gospel and money/possessions. In the last half of Matthew 6, Jesus is very clear: His followers are not to *seek* money and possessions, and neither are they to *worry* about them.

No doubt this teaching made its way from Jesus to the disciples and then to the early church. When they latched onto this revolutionary, countercultural perspective on earthly treasure, the residual effect was an economically diverse church. And if the church of Jesus Christ is to experience a reversion back to normal, biblical normal, we must use the gospel to exterminate the weeds of greed and materialism that threaten our souls. Silence is no longer an option.

For those of us who are leaders of the church of Jesus Christ in America, I think we share the joyful obligation of prophetically calling out the spirit of greed and materialism that is so pervasive among our people. No, we don't legalistically or self-righteously say what people can or cannot drive—that vision is too low. Instead we point out the absolute foolishness of investing in earthly treasure, lifting their gaze higher to heavenly treasure. We must stand and plead with our people that to put your faith in homes, cars, clothes, savings accounts, and college funds is foolish indeed.

Please don't hear me saying that saving is foolish and irresponsible. Instead, what each of us must constantly ask ourself is, "Am I saving or hoarding?" As a husband and father of three young boys, I naturally feel the need to provide. God expects me to take care of my family. A part of my provision involves saving for emergency situations, putting money away toward their college fund, and even thinking about providing after my death (Proverbs 13:22). The Scriptures take the mandate to provide so seriously that Paul writes, "But if anyone does not provide for his relatives, and especially for members of his household, he has denied the faith and is worse than an unbeliever" (1 Timothy 5:8).

There's a fine line between saving and hoarding. Saving has to do with providing for the needs of oneself and family and is therefore responsible. Hoarding is a completely different matter. We have crossed the line from saving to hoarding when our security is found in the amount of zeroes in the bank account, or when we are putting away not just to provide for the needs of our family but to provide for our greeds.

The Poor Helping the Poor

I am thankful for those Christians with limited resources who have learned to also provide for the needs of others. They continue to give generously out of their poverty. In fact, that is how my mother met the Savior one summer.

Karen grew up in the ghettoes of Philadelphia. Whatever image you have in your mind of life in the hood, multiply that by ten, and you have the environment my mother grew up in. She was born to a single-parent, teenage mother who wrestled with her own demons of addiction and was physically and emotionally abusive to my mother. One image that Karen carries with her was seeing her mom come home drunk on Saturday nights, and in the middle of her stupor demanding that my mother—her daughter—get her two brothers ready for church in the morning, while she stayed home to sleep off the hangover. This hypocrisy eventually would lead to my mother's salvation.

The sight of three kids walking to church on a Sunday morning without parental supervision definitely caught people's attention. One woman would have such compassion on my mother that she would pay for her to go to camp with all the other kids over the summer. With my grandmother's approval, Karen headed off to the woods—a scary place for a girl used to concrete and sirens. One night at camp a preacher came and "gave the gospel." Karen, feeling the tug of the Spirit, gave her life to Jesus, beginning the transformation.

When life took its abusive turns, my mother had someone to hold on to, someone who could bring order to her chaos. When she could take it no longer, she left the streets of Philadelphia to be reunited with her estranged father. A few months later he died of a sudden heart attack. Though still a young girl, Karen had a Savior who helped her navigate her grief. And today Karen Loritts—my mother—speaks all over the world, both proclaiming the gospel with her mouth and helping to bring order to the chaotic worlds of abused and battered women through a ministry she's started. My mother is having an astounding impact, because a woman opened her wallet and paid for her to go to camp.

"Someone's Child"

A gospel vision should not only focus us on heavenly things; it must compel us—and our children—to help humanity. We must restore an accurate biblical anthropology. What I mean by this is that until we see humanity the way God does, as being fearfully and wonderfully made in His image, we will not experience economic diversity in our churches and lives.

When I was a teenager I went with my father to Chicago. The years have faded my memory as to why we were there. The only thing I can remember is it being in the dead of winter. Winter in Chicago is nothing nice. The wind was howling this particular day as we walked down Michigan Avenue. I can still see the homeless man inadequately dressed, huddled against a corner of a building and trying desperately to shield himself from the wind. In his hand is a Styrofoam cup that he's poking out begging for money. I walk past him thinking that he's just going to hustle us, taking the money to inject some chemical substance in his body. My father, meanwhile, stops and places some money in the cup, encouraging him.

Dad then catches up to me, grabs me by the arm, and with tears welling up in his eyes he points back to the man and says, "Do you see him, Son? That man is someone's child! Some woman birthed him. At some point he had an address."

What my father was reminding me was that man was not some nameless, faceless, soulless person. That man is my brother!

A correct understanding of God and the Scriptures moves us toward compassion, forcing us to see the family of humanity—to see that all of us are bonded to one another, because all of us have been made in the image and likeness of God, regardless of our spiritual state. That man holding a sign at the busy intersection that says, "Will work for food," is my brother.

> "Do you see him, Son? That man is someone's child! Some woman birthed him."

That single mother working two jobs trying to make ends meet is my sister! That high school dropout standing on the street corner so desperate that he takes to a life of crime is family. Lose that vision and we will never engage them.

This vision of the family of humanity never left William Wilberforce. As a twenty-five-year-old white Member of Parliament, he had the nerve to stand up for the rights of poor black slaves. His concern and care for them was so astounding that most of his colleagues were repulsed. And yet, it was exactly this God-sized vision of the slaves being made in the image of God that compelled him to fight for their freedom and rights to the day he died.

Well-Meaning Efforts

We must be careful, though. If our understanding of the gospel and socioeconomic diversity stops here, we will drift off into paternalism. We can feel superior and have an attitude that condescends as we help others. Yes, we'll give our money and help those less fortunate, but a paternalistic attitude cannot take down the fences of class. In fact, it will actually strengthen them.

I once worked at a very large African-American church in Los Angeles. Because we were located in an impoverished community, members of well-meaning and wealthy suburban churches regularly asked if they could come and help. While we gladly received them, their generosity did nothing to foster an economically diverse environment. Their trips were all the same.

They'd spend the working week (usually their spring or summer breaks) tutoring kids, or helping to restore someone's home, and then their time would be capped off by coming to service on Sunday morning. Afterward I'd have to endure the all too familiar comments, "Wow, your music was really great" or, "Man this was the longest service of our lives!"

> While we appreciated their help, it came across like they were taking a weeklong trip to the zoo where they could look up close at a different demographic.

I have to confess that the prevailing feeling was that while we appreciated their help, it came across like they were taking a weeklong trip to the zoo where they could look up close at a different demographic, and yet always retreat back behind the fences of their comfortable lives, glad they were not among "the less fortunate." While I can't cast judgment on what was going on their hearts, it felt as if we were nothing more than people to be helped. There was no sense of brotherhood or family.

The Attitude of the Good Samaritan

Jesus railed against this in His classic parable of the good Samaritan. In essence, Jesus said that a man had been robbed and beaten. There he is, lying on the road, while two prominent Jews simply pass by him. The only one who stops is someone society considered to be a lowly person—a Samaritan. He tends to the man, puts the injured man up in a hotel, and offers to reimburse the innkeeper for any additional costs of restoring the wounded man back to health (Luke 10:29–36). And yet the most telling part of this amazing story is the reason why Jesus gives it. He tells this story in response to a lawyer's question, "Who is my neighbor?"

Notice the word *neighbor*. The question is not simply who should I help, or who should I take on as some sort of a project. But who is my neighbor? Laced in this term are themes of equality and brotherhood, not paternalism—a top-down mind-set.

The simple truth is, we will never build economically diverse lives or churches until we come to esteem all people as our neighbors. This is what Jesus profoundly understood and preached: that the gospel absolutely compels us to see people the way God does. Anything less than this dilutes the gospel of Jesus Christ. It is only when I understand the beauty of a rich God who has embraced a destitute sinner like myself, esteeming me as family, that I can in turn embrace those who are impoverished and destitute as family as well!

Vince Comes to Church

This is the message that we preach at our church here in Memphis. Our commitment to live out the gospel in all of its dimensions has compelled us to ask the question, "How can we create an environment where rich and poor can come together as neighbors?" This drives our thinking when it comes to location, how we put our community groups together, and many of the messages that we preach. And so far God has blessed our efforts.

Vince attends our church regularly. He started coming because he heard that those who helped to set up before service on Sunday nights (the time we were meeting then) could get free pizza. Being homeless and hungry, he jumped at the chance (plus it was our version of leaving margins in the field for the Vinces of the world to come and "glean"). Sunday after Sunday Vince would show up to work then eat. During this time he got to know a lot of people, and through the course of conversation we found out that he was walking about five or so miles to come to church. This led to people picking him up and taking him home. In giving him rides, people found out that Vince didn't have a social security number, was an alcoholic, and was unemployed. Concerned for Vince, a group of people helped him through a process of getting him a social security number, and put him in a treatment program where he has been sober for about three years now.

Today he is employed. I was joking with Vince the other Sunday about the fact that he'd put on a good amount of weight since sobering up, and we had a good laugh. Then he grabbed my hand, looked me in the eyes, and said, "Pastor, I want to thank you. This is the only place in my entire life that I've ever truly felt at home."

Is there a place for going down to the rescue mission and feeding the hungry? Absolutely. Is it wrong to do the annual Thanksgiving food drive? Not at all. But if this is all we're doing, and we're not creating an environment where the gospel is nudging people to get out of a "help" mentality and calling people to see everyone—including the poor—as their neighbors, then we are in danger of deepening the walls of class division. Instead, let's knock down those walls, cross to the other side of the tracks, and welcome our neighbors, just as Jesus commanded and gave us the example to follow.

6 THE GOSPEL AND THE GLORY OF GOD

If a man has a why for living,
he can stand almost any *how*.

Viktor Frankl

During a recent summer vacation up the East Coast, our family made a planned pit stop in Atlanta, my childhood home. While there I decided to call up some of my buddies at the last minute to see if they were in the mood to hang out. Excited that all of them could do it, I hopped in the car and headed for the downtown restaurant where we had agreed to meet.

Laughter filled the air that night as we reminisced about the foolishness of youth and the downright stupid things we did—like the times I would make my brother break-dance in a little back room at our church in between Sunday school and the worship service, charging people a quarter to see him do the Worm. The fun continued as we laughed at each other's increasing waist sizes and receding hairlines. Our conversation took a turn for the serious as we talked about the challenge of marriage and parenting. I guess this was the best time for one of our buddies to say that parenting was going to be even trickier now that he and his wife were getting divorced.

His revelation was like a thunderstorm on a sunny day.

His announcement struck all of us, but the news was especially hard for me to hear. I was there the day he met his soon-to-be wife. We were seminary roommates for two years, and along the way there were a lot of late-night conversations as I helped him navigate the tricky landscape of dating. When he was ready to get married, I took him to the same jeweler where I had just purchased my bride's ring. We were married within weeks of each other and spent the early formative years of marriage encouraging one another. His loss felt like it was my own.

I can't say I was surprised, though. Looking back, there were some huge warning signs—the biggest being when they both decided to renounce the faith and become agnostics. This came as a response to a legalistic church they joined, where week in and week out his wife was reprimanded by the older women in the church. One week she was scolded because she wasn't wearing her head covering. The next week it was because she had on pants. The next she had neglected her sweater, and now her back and tattoos were exposed. Legalism killed their spirits, and so they turned their back on God and the church, and tried to figure things out for a while. Unable to find their footing, they tumbled head-first and eyes wide-open into agnosticism. The final straw came when they filed for divorce.

As our evening was about to close, I had to ask my dear friend if he thought there was a connection between renouncing the gospel and the demise of his marriage. Without hesitating, he agreed his renouncing Christ made divorce likely. Without their core commitment to the gospel and without the help of other Christians, their marriage slipped into the abyss.

Sometimes we can conclude that the church, not the individual, bears sole responsibility for living the gospel. At times distinguishing the church from the individual can become biblically problematic; yet keep in mind that we each bear a personal responsibility to live out the gospel in all of its dimensions. That's the message of the previous three chapters. And as I discovered with my college friend, failing to embrace the gospel has consequences both for the church and the individual.

The Ultimate Goal: The Glory of God

Gospel living is done ultimately for the glory of God. We don't embrace the gospel for personal benefits. Following Jesus for what He can give us is to take the place of God in our lives, and commit the sins of idolatry and pride. What cannot be denied, though, is that embracing the gospel does yield rich fruit in our lives. I want to spend this chapter looking at three things that will flourish in our lives when we personally commit ourselves to living the gospel.

In Matthew 9:1–8 we meet a man who is simply described as being a paralytic. Like most of the people whom Jesus healed, we know little to nothing about the individual, not even their names. As odd as this may seem, it actually fits that we know hardly anything about this paralytic, or other recipients of Jesus' miracles, because these stories of deliverance aren't really about the person, but the glory of God.

What we know is this: The paralyzed man received the double blessing of being delivered from sin and being physically healed. Finally the text concludes with the response of the eyewitnesses that day: "He rose and went home. When the crowds saw it, they were afraid, and they *glorified* God, who had given such authority to men" (verses 7–8, emphasis added).

The punch line of the story is not the miracle, nor the person who received it—it's the glory of God. This story is not given to you and me to be in awe of the once paralyzed man who can now walk, but this story is given

> God often uses our felt needs to drive us to our greater needs.

to us that we might glorify—that is, make much of—the God of heaven and earth!

But what is this miracle's connection to the gospel? Let's take a look.

The first thing Jesus pronounces on this paralytic is the forgiveness of sins (verse 2). Jesus' words are troubling on multiple fronts; after all, the paralytic didn't come here to have his spiritual condition addressed, just his lifeless legs. If I'm the paralytic and I hear that my sins are forgiven, I couldn't help but feel somewhat disappointed as I look at my legs then back at Jesus, trying to subtly imply that I'm there for a much different reason. Actually, it makes sense. God often uses our felt needs to drive us to our greater needs.

My wife and I speak at marriage conferences for the Family Life ministry. Even though our ministry is based on the Scriptures and God's blueprint for marriage, both Christ-followers and those who are not even interested in Jesus attend these conferences. What drives the non-Christ-followers to these conferences is that many of them feel their marriages are paralyzed (as do some Christians). But by the end of the weekend, many of the non-Christian couples with "immobile" marriages have given their hearts to Jesus. Their felt needs became the pathway to get them to their greatest need—the forgiveness of sins and a precious Savior, Jesus Christ.

Such is the experience of the paralytic—before he gets physical healing, he gets heaven when Jesus says that his sins are forgiven. To the religious leaders who observe the interaction, Jesus' doling out forgiveness is especially troublesome. Our text tells us that the scribes react to Jesus' words by thinking that He is blaspheming, since forgiving sins is something only God could do, right? This is *exactly* Jesus' point. When He forgives the paralytic of his sins, Jesus is saying that He—the Son of Man—is God (see verse 6). It is an incredible statement affirming His deity. Having forgiven the paralytic's sin, Jesus connects this man vertically with God.

The horizontal dimensions of the gospel are seen in this story as well. At the end of verse 6 Jesus tells him to, "Rise, pick up your bed and go home." The bed that Jesus was referring to was the social and cultural equivalent of our wheelchair. This was where the paralytic stayed as he begged people for money. Now that his legs are restored, he has no need for his wheelchair, yet think of the implications. He can no longer beg and posture himself as a consumer in his city. With his legs repaired he has no excuse; he must go and get a job and become a positive contributor to his society, aiding in the welfare of the city. He's now restored horizontally to the community.

Having seen the gospel in Matthew 9:1–8, we're now ready to revisit the purpose for Jesus saving this man and restoring him as a key player to his community—nothing less than the glory of God. The community is in awe of God as this man folds up his "wheelchair" and pushes it out of the room, heading to look for employment. The gospel ends with the glory of God.

Happiness and Holiness

In a very individualistic society like America, it would be more popular for me to present the gospel as: "Jesus came to die to make your life better . . . or more peaceful . . . or to make you more happy." Are there some residual benefits that come from following Jesus? Sometimes, but ultimately we don't follow Jesus for the benefits or blessings; we cling to the gospel for the glory of God.

As I write these words Korie and I are anxiously awaiting the results of her biopsy. My sweet wife has three swollen lymph nodes in her neck, and we've been waiting all week to find out if she has cancer or not. Leaving the doctor's office where I just watched them stick a needle in her neck four times to get enough tissue, I found my mind reverting back to Matthew 9:1–8, where the paralytic gets his sins forgiven and then gets his legs healed. I asked myself the question, *What if all the paralytic got that day was the forgiveness of his sins and never got his legs healed? Would heaven be enough?* I then had to make it personal: *Bryan, what if your wife does have cancer and you watch her suffer in the months to come? Is heaven enough? What if God is trusting us with cancer so that we might glorify Him all the more, and she never gets her physical healing on this side of heaven? Is heaven enough?* I have to conclude that the gospel is not about finding meaning in my life, or forgiving others (we'll talk about those two coming up), as much as it is about the glory of God.

In his wonderful book *Sacred Marriage*, Gary Thomas wonders aloud, Is marriage more about *our* holiness than *our* happiness? His question is profound and needed, but I don't think he goes far enough, for in his questions Thomas still places the individual at the center of marriage; but the gospel says we're not the center, God is. When we see the glory of God as the apex of the gospel, and not our happiness or holiness, that changes everything . . . everything!

The problem with life, someone once said, is that it's so daily. We tend to lose the bigger picture. What the glory of God provides us with is that higher perspective. My wife has been given to me for one purpose— to so love, cherish, and lead that I display the glory of God. My children have been graciously given to me to so nurture, care for, and lead that I might display the glory of God. Work is a gift not to make money ultimately but that I might display the surpassing beauty of God. The gospel enables us to display the surpassing infinite value of God!

> The question is never "Do we worship?" but "What or who are we worshiping?"

The "Why" for Living

But there's other things that the gospel provides the Christ-follower. In Romans 1 Paul helps us to see that worship is universal. He points out that we either worship the creation or the Creator. When we give glory and honor to the Creator through times of worship, we make a divine connection. At its core, worship is the longing of the soul to connect with someone or something greater than itself.

It's through the act of worship that we find fulfillment and meaning in life. Because everyone worships, idolatry is also universal, because idolatry is worship. Our hearts are idol factories where we long to ascribe ultimate value to people and things outside of God. Everyone worships. The question is never "Do we worship?" but "What or who are we worshiping?"

Why is this? Solomon helps us when he writes that God "has put eternity into man's heart" (Ecclesiastes 3:11). Our hearts have a built-in dissatisfaction with merely the things of this life. Maybe we are satisfied with our idols for a season, but over time we are never fully satisfied for our idols will never truly scratch where our soul itches.

Viktor Frankl's classic, *Man's Search for Meaning*, gives us a glimpse of this. A trained psychiatrist and also a prisoner in a Nazi concentration camp, Frankl was fascinated at how some Jews were able to deal with the horrors of the Holocaust, while others were mentally crushed under its weight. He concluded, "If a man has a *why* for living, he can stand almost any *how*."[1] Humanity desperately needs transcendent meaning in order to feel stable during the unsettling moments in life. If Frankl had been seated with my friends in that Atlanta restaurant that summer, he would have concluded that once my friend and his wife stripped away their *why* for living, they never had a chance when the bumpy *hows* of life came up.

The hope of the Christ-follower is that man's ultimate why for living is found in the cross and the empty tomb—where Jesus died in my place for my sins, was buried, and then rose three days later. True, lasting meaning in life cannot be found outside of the atonement of Jesus and the new life that He provides. In one of His classic paradoxical statements, Jesus said to His followers, "Whoever finds his life will lose it, and whoever loses his life for my sake will find it" (Matthew 10:39). True life, a life rich with meaning, can only come when we die to the idols of this world, embrace the gospel, and follow Jesus.

When Two Rich Men Searched for Meaning

Two stories, one old, the other recent, tell about two rich men who eventually realized money is not the goal nor the fulfillment to life. One of the most visible places in the Bible where Jesus shows us the futility of seeking satisfaction in this life apart from the gospel is in His conversation with an individual described in three Gospels as being a rich young ruler (Mark 10: 17–22; see also Matthew 19:22; Luke 18:18). Mark writes:

> As he was setting out on his journey, a man ran up and knelt before him and asked him, "Good Teacher, what must I do to inherit eternal life?" And Jesus said to him, "Why do you call me good? No one is good except God alone. You know the commandments: Do not murder, Do not commit adultery, Do not steal, Do not bear false witness, Do not defraud, Honor your father and mother." And he said to him, "Teacher, all these I have kept from my youth." And Jesus, looking at him, loved him, and said to him, "You lack one thing: go, sell all that you have and give to the poor, and you will have treasure in heaven; and come, follow me." Disheartened by the saying, he went away sorrowful, for he had great possessions." (10:17–22)

This man is wealthy. The last verse tells us that this man had "great possessions." He's also religious. When Jesus tells him to keep the commandments and then spells out what they are, the man replies that he has not only kept these commandments, but he's done so from his youth. Yet in spite of his wealth and his religious observance, he's still extremely dissatisfied. His coming to Jesus and asking how he can inherit eternal life betrays the unrest of his soul despite his wealth and religion.

The second rich man appears in the recent sequel to the popular 1980s movie *Wall Street*. Gordon Gecko, a corporate raider and multimillionaire, has just been released from jail after serving time for securities fraud.

After some manipulation, he comes into a hundred million dollars and resumes his seat of power. As he stands at the tailor's shop being measured for another custom-made suit, there's the satisfaction on his face at the thought that his life finally has experienced some sense of redemption and meaning.

That feeling is short-lived, though, because his estranged daughter is pregnant. When Gecko sees the ultrasound, he's seated behind his big desk, the very picture of power and prestige. Looking at the picture, he realizes that he will never see his grandchild, and no amount of money can fix this longing in his soul. The picture says it all; power, prestige and money cannot give transcendent meaning in life, nor can religion, only the gospel of Jesus Christ.

Meanwhile, the Gospel writer Mark notes how Jesus offers the rich young ruler a way off the treadmill of meaninglessness. Jesus tells him to sell all of his possessions, give to the poor, and *follow Him*. Never content to expose the problem, Jesus offers the solution by saying that the pathway to meaning is through the gospel (Mark 10:21).

How does Jesus depict the gospel during their encounter? Jesus asks the rich man to give his money to the poor, thus showing the horizontal dimension of the gospel. Jesus then tells him, "Come, follow me." Here we see the vertical dimensions of the gospel—living in relationship with God through His Son, Jesus Christ. When we live the gospel in both dimensions, we experience the by-product of a life rich with meaning.

Meaning through Sacrifice

The most meaningful things in life come at the greatest cost. There is a direct relationship between sacrifice and meaning. Several years ago my wife and I were talking about death, and she asked me where I wanted to be buried. This was a great question because I've lived in six different states. After thinking for a few moments, I told her to bury me in Memphis. When she asked me why, I responded that this was the place that means the most to me. We came here with twenty-six people longing to reach the city with a gospel-centered, multiethnic church. Years of hard work filled with sacrifice has resulted in deep satisfaction. Memphis has not been the most comfortable of situations, but it has been the most meaningful.

I guess that's why the gospel's emblem is the cross. Through Jesus' torturous and bloody death on the cross flow deep rivers of fulfillment. It is through the ultimate payment of death that the greatest treasures this life will ever know are granted. King Solomon understood this. Though he did not use the language of the cross, he did speak of the antithesis of meaning when he talked constantly in the book of Ecclesiastes about futility, or meaninglessness. Surveying all of the amenities that were available to him, he said:

> I said in my heart, "Come now, I will test you with pleasure; enjoy yourself." But behold, this also was vanity. . . . I made great works. I built houses and planted vineyards for myself. I made myself gardens and parks, and planted in them all kinds of fruit trees. I made myself pools from which to water the forest of growing trees. I bought male and female slaves, and had slaves who were born in my house. I had also great possessions of herds and flocks, more than any who had been before me in Jerusalem. I also gathered for myself silver and gold and the treasure of kings and provinces. I got singers, both men and women, and many concubines, the delight of the children of man.
>
> So I became great and surpassed all who were before me in Jerusalem. Also my wisdom remained with me. And whatever my eyes desired I did not keep from them. I kept my heart from no pleasure, . . . Then I considered all that my hands had done and the toil I had expended in doing it, and behold, all was vanity and a striving after wind, and there was nothing to be gained under the sun. (Ecclesiastes 2:1, 4–11)

Solomon took inventory of his life, and you would think that the houses, women, possessions, and his position as king would bring ultimate fulfillment, but instead Solomon said it brought vanity. Writing his thoughts originally in Hebrew, the word translated as *vanity* actually means *emptiness*. Stuff, Solomon says, didn't satisfy.

Had Solomon been born centuries later and encountered Christ, Jesus would have told him the same thing He said to the rich young man: sell all you have and give to the poor, then follow Me; live the gospel, for this is the pathway to meaning.

Who knows what ended up happening to the rich young man. Maybe he did listen to Jesus some years later; we'll never know until our heavenly life begins. If he did hold onto his possessions trying desperately to be satisfied by them, we won't have to guess at his deathbed confession: his last words would be an echo of Solomon's, "Behold, all was vanity and striving after wind, and there was nothing to be gained under the sun."

A life of meaning awaits those who follow the way of the cross. It is a path of sacrifice and discomfort (see chapter 8), but it leads us to great fulfillment as we honor the Father of forgiveness and God of all comfort.

A Life of Forgiveness

Living the gospel in all of its dimensions will provide Christ-followers with a way to glorify God and a life of true meaning, but there's more. It will also push us to forgive, thus promoting rich and vibrant relationships with others. While it may seem as if forgiveness is not that big of a deal in connection with the gospel, we should think again. As my grandmother was prone to say, "We don't live in heaven and board down here." When God saved us He didn't beckon us home; instead He left us here, recipients of His gospel, to live it in the context of a world filled with evil. Given the reality of sin and evil in our world, forgiveness, and a large helping of it, is a necessity for the follower of Jesus Christ. In fact, not to forgive is a failure to live the gospel.

Jesus Himself connects forgiveness with the gospel. He tells the story of a servant who had fallen into so much debt that he was unable to pay his master. He knows that justice requires him to be thrown in jail. With no resources to fall on, the servant does the only thing he can think to do; he drops to his knees and begs his master to forgive him (Matthew 18: 23–27).

It works! Without setting up a payment plan, the master, in an astounding act of forgiveness, releases him of his debt.

The story now takes a turn as this just forgiven servant goes out and finds a fellow servant who owes him an amount much less than what he owed his master. Refusing to forgive him, the first servant beats the man without mercy, even choking him, all the while demanding that payment would be made.

When word gets back to this servant's master, he's irate. How could this man, whom he had just forgiven, go out and refuse forgiveness on someone who owed him a far less amount? So the master takes the unmerciful servant and gives him his just due by throwing him in jail and forcing him to repay.

No doubt, for anyone standing in the crowd that day, they would have gotten the point long before Jesus drew it out. For a person to receive forgiveness demands that we display forgiveness to one another; failure to do so is the epitome of hypocrisy. Jesus ends His story of the unforgiving servant with these words, "So also my heavenly Father will do to every one of you, if you do not forgive your brother from your heart" (Matthew 18:35).

"My Forgiveness Is Real"

Hidden in this story is the gospel. Like both servants, all of us have accrued an incredible debt with God. Our sins have put us in the red. Yet in an incredible act of grace, "God shows his love for us in that while we were still sinners, Christ died for us" (Romans 5:8). The good news of the gospel is that when we could not pay our debts and deserved an eternity in hell, God mercifully paid them by sacrificing His one and only Son,

Jesus Christ. The gospel is both justice and mercy.

When I went to seminary, I had no clue how school would get paid for. I had applied for scholarships but had received no answer when it was time to pack my little car and drive to school. So I journeyed almost three thousand miles across country, just trusting God to provide. Not long after arriving on campus, I got word that I had received a scholarship that was specifically designed for people who could not afford to pay for seminary, people like me. The tears rolled down my face when I read that I would not have to pay a dime for school. The debt had mercifully been paid.

> To forgive is to be like God; to withhold forgiveness is to be like the world.

However, scholarships are not the ignoring of the cost. Justice demanded that the costs associated with me attending be paid. While I didn't have to pay them, the debt was satisfied, just through someone else. This is justice.

The gospel demands that the debts we accrued with God get paid. Jesus raised His hand and said that He'd be our scholarship; He would satisfy the debt. What justice, but also what mercy. In an incredible act of mercy and forgiveness, Jesus does for us what we could never do for ourselves—He satisfies the demands and wrath of God.

All who have received such mercy and forgiveness are now obligated to be dispensers of forgiveness to others. The gospel demands that just as I have vertically received the forgiveness of God on my behalf, that I now lavish forgiveness horizontally on others. The gospel woos us to forgive. Jesus' story in Matthew 18 tells us that one of the distinctive marks of a life that embraces the cross of Jesus and the gospel, is that we forgive.

One of the most visible witnesses to the world that God is in us, that we are truly living the gospel, is when we forgive. Because we've vertically received the forgiveness of God, this same forgiveness is to rush out of us and into the world, releasing those who have violated us. To forgive is to be like God; to withhold forgiveness is to be like the world.

When Nelson Mandela became the leader of South Africa, he was dealing with a nation that had been ravaged by apartheid, a political and social system that elevated whites over blacks and kept the two groups separate. The two peoples desperately needed to be reconciled to one another. How would this happen? Mandela decided to set up the Truth and Reconciliation Commission. His infamous TRC hearings brought together whites and blacks, oppressors and oppressed. People would confess their sinful acts at the hearings and receive forgiveness.

At one such hearing a white police officer confessed that during apartheid he and other officers came to a black woman's home, shot her eighteen-year-old son, and burned his body. Eight years later the policeman and his friends returned to take this same woman's husband, tying him up with ropes, dousing him with gasoline, and setting him on fire as they made her watch as he screamed horrifically to his death. Hearing such gratuitous violence caused an audible hush to fall on the hearing.

How would this woman respond? What would she say to this man who had killed her husband and only child? She made two requests of him. One was that she would be honored if he could take her to the spot where he burned her husband's body, so that she could gather the dirt and provide a decent burial for him. With head down, he nodded in agreement. Then the woman looked at him and said that she still had a lot of love to give, and would be pleased if he could come to her home twice a month so she could cook for him and "be a mother to him." She added, "I would like to embrace him so he can know my forgiveness is real."[2] Out of nowhere people in the hearing began to sing, "Amazing Grace." They were simply overwhelmed by this woman's act of forgiveness.

Forgiveness is irrational. What makes the most sense is to settle the score, to get even, or to put up walls and ignore, all the while refusing to release the debtor of the offense. But when you're infected with the gospel, your relationships are affected radically. Given the otherworldly quality of forgiveness, it's no wonder that Jesus connects it to the gospel. The gospel becomes the only operating system that will propel us to generously forgive, again and again.

7 DECLARING THE WHOLE TRUTH

Civil War veteran Colonel Heine once said
that Lincoln "had the honor of signing the
land-grants of the greatest railroad of the
world with the same pen that had
decreed the abolishment of slavery."

Much of this book so far has been about what's missing, or *The Hole in the Gospel,* as Richard Stearns puts it. Yet we can't stop here. We've got to get to the solution side of things. Our search for the missing ingredients to the gospel takes us back to the Scriptures, where God articulates Himself very clearly.

My aim in this chapter is simple—to spotlight the passages of Scripture and biblical examples that point to the core truth that the gospel is *both* my relationship with God *and* my relationship with others.

Evidence from the Old Testament

The gospel is not a strictly New Testament doctrine. Sure, its ultimate climax and fulfillment comes in the person of Jesus Christ, and His finished work on the cross when He died in our place and for our sins, but the Old Testament gives us (as it so often does) glimpses of the gospel. One of the first traces of the gospel we see in the Scriptures is found in Genesis 12:1–3:

Now the Lord said to Abram, "Go from your country and your kindred and your father's house to the land that I will show you. And I will make of you a great nation, and I will bless you and make your name great, so that you will be a blessing. I will bless those who bless you, and him who dishonors you I will curse, and in you all the families of the earth shall be blessed."

This passage is commonly referred to as the Abrahamic covenant, because it marks the beginnings of God's covenantal relationship with not only Abraham (named Abram in our passage; God will later change his name to Abraham) but his offspring, the nation of Israel. Here God gathers a people to Himself, calling them into relationship with Him. Because Genesis 12:1–3 involves God's covenantal relationship with His people, we can say that it gives us a glimpse of the gospel.

But what specifically about the gospel does Genesis 12:1–3 show us? The Abrahamic covenant reveals to us the vertical dimensions of the gospel in that God calls the Jews to Himself, but we also see the horizontal dimensions of the gospel when God ends the covenant by saying that "in you all the families of the earth shall be blessed." Here we see God's heart not just for a specific people group (the Jews) but for the whole world (all the *families* of the earth). God longed to use the nation of Israel as a vehicle to bless and transform the world.

As we walk through the Old Testament, we see examples of this. A Jewish man named Joseph is used to bless Egypt by helping the Egyptian people navigate a famine. Another Jew named Daniel influences a Gentile leader named Nebuchadnezzar in Daniel chapter 4, helping to lead him to faith in God. Later on the Jewish prophet Jonah is unwillingly used to usher in revival to his pagan oppressors, the nation of Assyria.

It is only when the nation of Israel is walking with God that we see her as an instrument of blessing to the people around her. This is a herald of the gospel.

Evidence from the Ministry of Jesus

Jesus devoted His public ministry to teaching and living the gospel. His preaching centered on inviting people to "repent, for the kingdom of heaven is at hand" (Matthew 3:2; 4:17). The message of repentance was one Jesus preached many times, and as a result many people were vertically connected with God.

Jesus' message of repentance was not a very controversial one in His day; after all, His cousin John preached it as well, with hardly anyone objecting. What got Jesus in trouble was the notion that the kingdom of heaven was not just for the pious Jews, but it was also for moral lepers like tax collectors and prostitutes. His dining with tax collectors, conversing with immoral women, and allowing Himself to be touched by prostitutes ignited a firestorm of objection that, along with His claim to be God, ultimately led to His death on the cross. Yet herein lies the beauty of the cross, for it's through the blood and shame of it that a new community could be created where the orthodox and immoral can sit side by side, embracing one another. This is what Jesus envisioned and labored toward. This is the gospel.

In His humanity, Jesus was a Jew; and as a Jewish man He would have been well acquainted with the Abrahamic covenant. In fact, Jesus would have seen Himself as the ultimate fulfillment of the covenant, for as the Jewish God-Man He would die on the cross, offering up His own body to bless all of those who would receive His sacrifice, both Jew and Gentile alike. It would be through Jesus that all of the nations would receive their ultimate blessing in being reconciled to God (vertically) and to one another (horizontally). In Jesus is the coming together of the vertical and the horizontal.

Examples from the First Church

In Acts 2, we continue to see the multifaceted dimensions of the gospel. It begins with Peter standing and preaching to thousands in

Jerusalem on the Day of Pentecost. Luke, the writer of Acts, is careful to show us that gathered in Jerusalem that day was a multiethnic community who were sympathetic to Judaism. He writes, "Now there was dwelling in Jerusalem Jews, devout men from every nation under heaven. And at this sound the multitude came together, and they were bewildered, because each one was hearing them speak in his own language" (verses 5–6). Peter stands and declares the gospel to this ethnically diverse gathering, and three thousand people enter into the new covenant by confessing their sins and claiming Jesus Christ as Lord.

Toward the end of Acts 2, Luke shows us something else about this new multiethnic community of faith:

> And they devoted themselves to the apostles' teaching and the fellowship, to the breaking of bread and the prayers. And awe came upon every soul, and many wonders and signs were being done through the apostles. And all who believed were together and had all things in common. And they were selling their possessions and belongings and distributing the proceeds to all, as any had need. (verses 42–45)

Look carefully at Luke's observation of the first church and you'll see that not only was it ethnically diverse, but it was economically diverse as well. We know this because Luke shows us that there were people who were in need ("as any had need"), and that there were people who had it to give, because they were able to sell their possessions and belongings. Later on, we see several members of the early church selling their fields, taking the proceeds, and laying it at the apostles' feet so that they could distribute to the poor within their church. Clearly, there was rich and poor worshiping side by side in the first church.

Against the backdrop of such diversity, Luke paints a picture of a community who was so moved by what God had done for the people that this love poured out in acts of service for one another. God's gracious gift of salvation stirred deep acts of benevolence among the community of faith toward each other. This is the gospel.

The Story of Philemon

While one of the shortest books in the Scriptures, the book of Philemon poses one of the biggest challenges for Christ-followers, because of the issue of slavery. In this letter, we encounter a slave named Onesimus who has run away from his owner, Philemon. Paul knew Philemon through his labors in the gospel, and sometime later came in contact with Onesimus, who had recently surrendered his heart to Jesus Christ.

I imagine that what happens next is one of the most drastic emotional swings in human history. Quite possibly Onesimus is beaming with joy as he shares with Paul his sheer delight in his new relationship with Jesus. He's growing leaps and bounds in his faith and is a portal of questions. Paul answers patiently, while maybe thinking at the same time, "I really don't want to tell him this . . . but I have to." Paul takes a deep breath and says to Onesimus that while he's excited for his conversion, he's got some news that Onesimus will not like—he has to return to his master, Philemon. His joy has been exchanged for gloom. This is the gospel too.

While we can get lost in the sociological questions that shroud Paul's instructions to Onesimus—and they are great questions to wrestle with, involving the institution of slavery—we must venture out above the haze and ask the bigger question: "How did Paul's understanding of the gospel influence his directive to Onesimus to go back to his master, Philemon?" For Paul the returning of a slave to his master was not some moral impulse that one gets when they find a twenty dollar bill that just flew out of a woman's purse on the ground, driving them to give it back to her. There's far more at stake.

Listen to what Paul says to Philemon as he pleads with him to take Onesimus back: "For this perhaps is why he was parted from you for a while, that you might have him back forever, no longer as a slave but more than a slave, as a beloved brother—especially to me, but how much more to you, both in the flesh and in the Lord" (15–16).

At stake here is the gospel. Since now both men are followers of Jesus Christ, having been reconciled to God, their newfound vertical relationship means a drastic paradigm shift in how they horizontally relate to one another. The gospel compels Onesimus to go back to Philemon, and this same gospel beckons Philemon to receive him back with open arms, embracing him as a dear brother in Christ. In the span of twenty-five verses, Paul is clear that the gospel has both vertical and horizontal implications.

Sin and the Gospel

So far our survey of the Scriptures has shown us that the gospel offers complete reconciliation by connecting humanity to God and to one another, offering whole new paradigms in relationships and hope for the future. But fundamentally, sin—the antithesis of the gospel—has wrecked the very thing that the gospel has come to repair: our relationship with God and others. When we contemplate the problem of sin, we'll only see the beauty of the gospel.

In the opening chapters of Genesis, we see Adam and Eve enjoying rich community with God. Daily they commune with their Creator. (I wonder what those conversations were like.) Their intimacy was such that Genesis 3:8 tells us that when they heard the *sound* of God walking, they hid themselves. There were a lot of things walking in the garden. Giraffes. Elephants. Deer. So how could they just hear a sound and be able to say, "Nope, that's not a monkey or a gazelle; that's God!" Adam and Eve must've walked with God so much that they could distinguish the sound of His gait from all others. Theirs was community in the most authentic sense.

But what happened that would cause these two individuals to withdraw from the One they had walked so closely with? Sin. Their decision to act independently of God placed a wedge in their vertical relationship with Him. What's more, that sin would pose a constant threat in their relationship with each other. God told Eve, "Your desire shall be for your husband, and he shall rule over you" (3:16b). Since then every relational problem can be accredited to sin. Sin has disconnected humanity from God and from one another. Sin kills relationships, while the gospel breathes new life into them.

How exactly do vibrant relationships with God and others continue, even after I have violated that person by sinning? God's provision for these inevitable breaches would be to establish a system of reconciliation founded on sacrifice. In other words, God said that if the relationship He shared with us has any hopes of living, something must die. In the Old Testament this something, this sacrifice, was an animal. Every time someone violated God by breaking His law, a sacrifice had to be offered. When someone had sinned against another human being, a sacrifice needed to be provided. Death was the paradoxical means of living and maintaining vibrant relationships.

In Matthew 5, Jesus says, "So if you are offering your gift at the altar and there remember that your brother has something against you, leave your gift there before the altar and go. First be reconciled to your brother, and then come and offer your gift" (23–24). If the gift or the sacrifice was meant to restore life into our vertical relationship with God and our horizontal relationship with others, then it would be hypocritical for me to offer a sacrifice and refuse to do all that I could to repair the relationship that's been broken with my brother.

> One of the legacies of the cross of Christ is that we have been knighted ministers of reconciliation.

Jesus' point is clear: to offer a sacrifice of any kind, while not experiencing the life-giving beauty of reconciled relationships, is to reduce the offering to a mere ritual, making us no better than the Pharisees.

At our church we take Communion every Sunday, pausing to reflect on the sacrifice that Jesus made for us in reconciling us to God and to one another. As I watch people come forward, my heart breaks some Sundays as I see husbands and wives on the brink of divorce, former friends giving each other the silent treatment, and other broken relationships taking the bread and the cup, the sacrifice of Jesus, yet continue to live in such horizontal brokenness. We Americans can easily rationalize this with our individualized worldview of life—*it really is about me and God*—but this is not a biblical perspective of the gospel. If in fact the gospel has everything to do with my relationship with God *and* my relationship with others, then for me to not feel a sense of urgency in reconciling with my brother and sister while I continue to tithe, attend church, or serve in ministry is to miss what the Bible from Genesis to Revelation has to say about the gospel—and it is to show a blatant disregard for the cross. Paul reminds the Corinthians that one of the legacies of the cross of Christ is that we have been knighted ministers of reconciliation (2 Corinthians 5:18).

Lincoln's Legacy

One of the great legacies of Abraham Lincoln, one of America's most beloved presidents, can be described in one word: *reconciliation*. Through his tireless efforts, President Lincoln led the charge to reunite people of the North and South.

While much has been made of Lincoln's leadership during the Civil War, not many realize that his legacy of reconciliation stretched east and west as well. It would be Lincoln who would set in motion the building of the transcontinental railroad, which would usher in decades of economic prosperity and transform the nation. Civil War veteran Colonel Heine once said that Lincoln "had the honor of signing the land-grants of the greatest railroad of the world with the same pen that had decreed the abolishment of slavery."[2]

The bringing together of North and South, East and West came at a great cost. Both the Civil War and the building of the transcontinental railroad cost many their lives. Lincoln himself would pay the highest price, as his own life would be prematurely taken by a deranged assassin. Our sixteenth president knew full well that bringing people together involves sacrifice.

For those of us who have been reconciled to God, and therefore to each other as well, being placed into the body of Christ, this act of reconciliation came through the sacrifice of Jesus Christ. His death would bring about the reconciliation of God and humanity—the north and the south. It also made possible the restoration of broken human relationships—the east with the west. And that is the gospel: the cross with its vertical beam of reconciliation with God and its horizontal beam of restored relationships with our fellow man.

This sacrifice of God's Son to reconcile us with God and restore our relationships with each other forms the scarlet thread woven throughout Scripture. This is the gospel of Jesus Christ.

GETTING COMFORTABLE WITH A LIFE OF DIS-EASE

8

> The strong must disadvantage themselves
> for the weak, the majority for
> the minority, or the community
> frays and the fabric breaks.
>
> Tim Keller

The English are not known for their culinary abilities, but they do have an international reputation for one particular dish. I guess that's why every time I visit England, I request what I never have in America—their staple of fish and chips. Sitting at a restaurant in London recently, enjoying a meal, I decided to share with friends on Twitter and Facebook what I was eating that evening. So I took out my phone, typed the maximum 140 characters, pushed a button, and instantly thousands of people as far away as California and the Middle East knew what Bryan Loritts was consuming for dinner. To an introvert, social media like Twitter is pure joy!

Twitter, of course, is used by all kinds of people for more than just updates. Many choose to give an inspiring thought or an encouraging "word" via social media. Pulling out my phone and scrolling through the most recent list of tweets, here's what some of the people I follow are saying:

"Feel beaten up? Remember scars don't form on the dead but on the living."

"No one can do everything about the suffering and unfairness in our world, but everyone can do something."

"Be a soldier today who doesn't blow his composure."

"Majority culture leader: steward white privilege for the sake of all."

All of these tweets contain an element of truth in them that is at least worth contemplating. But neither I nor the millions of others who use Twitter ever really stop and say we need to radically readjust our lives to what was just said in this tweet. While there are many descriptions for twitter, "life altering" is not one of them.

I don't think it's an overstatement to suggest that most of the people in the world pragmatically relate to the Bible as if it were a vast collection of tweets. We find the words of Scripture to be thought provoking and inspiring, yet most of us tend to resist applying its words to our lives. This response goes beyond those who are not followers of Jesus Christ—I find that even in my own experience there are certain sections of Scripture that I tend to view as pithy tweets. These are some of the statements in the Bible that I'd be a lot more comfortable with if they originated on someone's Twitter page:

"If anyone would come after me, let him deny himself and take up his cross and follow me."—Jesus (Matthew 16:24)

"Children, how difficult it is to enter the kingdom of God! It is easier for a camel to go through the eye of a needle than for a rich person to enter the kingdom of God."—Jesus (Mark 10:24–25)

"Whoever loves father or mother more than me is not worthy of me, and whoever loves son or daughter more than me is not worthy of me. And whoever does not take his cross and follow me is not worthy of me."—Jesus (Matthew 10:37–38)

"Do not love the world or the things in the world. If anyone loves the world, the love of the Father is not in him."—John (1 John 2:15)

The first three statements are by Jesus; the fourth by one of His followers, the apostle John. Along with every other writer and speaker in the Scriptures, John and Jesus were not competing with one another to see who could send out the catchiest statement so that it would be retweeted, and thus recruit more followers. Popularity was not their objective. Instead, their words are the epitome of the gospel, which is never satisfied with contemplation. The goal is radical life transformation.

This is important as we round third and head toward home in our discussion of the gospel. A lot has been said so far about the gospel's central message of reconciling sinners to God and to one another. The sacrifice of Jesus reminds us that the call to be Christ-followers is a call to a life of sacrifice, being misunderstood, and on occasion, times of great discomfort. A cross-shaped gospel involves a total revisioning of not only how we see the world but also how we navigate relationships. The gospel is hardly just another tweet.

We now wrestle with the question "How do I know that the gospel has invaded my life in deeply practical ways?" In this chapter we will

Discomfort is an essential part of Christianity.

discover that one of the obvious fruits of the gospel in the life of an individual is that he will never become comfortable with comfortable. The gospel nudges us to embrace a life of dis-ease. We'll see that Christianity was birthed in and came of age through discomfort, and because discomfort is an essential part of Christianity, any gospel that seeks to eliminate it from our lives is no gospel at all. Finally, we'll look at some very practical ways we can go to war with comfort in our lives.

A Culture of Comfort

Many American Christians in the twenty-first century live in an age of comfort. There's an old expression that says "to a worm in horseradish the world is horseradish."[1] If you want to sense my struggle in trying to explain to American Christians our culture of comfort, try to describe horseradish to the worm that's lived in it—it's all it knows.

As a pastor, I've learned that many of the people I shepherd have the misconception that I'm in the business of customer service, so they apply that slogan The Customer Is Always Right, which gives them license to complain. If you want a very interesting conversation with a Christian leader, ask the individual to tell you what people in their ministry or church have complained about over the years. You'll be in stitches and grieved all at once.

> In the pantheon of American gods, comfort is right near the top.

There's always complaints about music, from style to volume. "We're too contemporary" or "We're too traditional" . . . "The music's too loud (or too soft)." There's the concern about doing Communion so often that it becomes ritualistic, to not doing it enough. Others have wondered why our church doesn't offer a gluten-free option for Communion. (No, I'm not kidding.) To some the service is too long; to others the parking too congested or the drivers too mean. All of these are actual complaints that I've experienced from people who call themselves followers of Jesus, and all center around the area of comfort.

Then there is the constant struggle to get people to serve in the church . . . for one hour on Sunday. Currently, our volunteer base is about one-third of those who call our church home, which means two-thirds of our people don't serve. Frustrated, I called several of my pastor friends, and to a man they all said I'm doing good to get such a "high" percentage.

Our poor children's ministry workers get treated like a herd of tele-marketers when they try to recruit people to serve twice a month for a total of two hours. Finally, when people do agree to serve, it's not uncommon to have them either not show or show up late and so disgruntled it seems as if we've ruined their weekends.

All of this leads me to wonder that if members can't "sacrifice" an hour a week on Sundays, can these same people take up their cross and follow Jesus the other six days of the week? In the pantheon of American gods, comfort is right near the top, even in the church.

The Importance of Dis-Ease

Those in the early church understood that Christianity was birthed and enmeshed in this whole idea of dis-ease. Jesus taught the necessity of taking up one's cross. What's more, Jesus modeled the idea of ultimate sacrificial service by dying on one. Most of the twelve disciples followed His example by giving their lives as martyrs. Beyond their leaders, the church at large experienced severe helpings of discomfort. Consider the words of the writer of Hebrews as he wrote to a group of Christians:

> But recall the former days when, after you were enlightened, you endured a hard struggle with sufferings, sometimes being publicly exposed to reproach and affliction, and sometimes being partners with those so treated. For you had compassion on those in prison, and you joyfully accepted the plundering of your property, since you knew that you yourselves had a better possession and an abiding one. Therefore do not throw away your confidence, which has a great reward. For you have need of endurance, so that when you have done the will of God you may receive what is promised. (Hebrews 10:32–36)

See the dis-ease in their lives: "hard struggle" . . . "publicly exposed" . . . "affliction" . . . "prison." These are hardly words of comfort. In fact, what is described here, with all its intensity, was actually normal for the first-century follower of Jesus. Discomfort was a way of life for most believers of that era. What's more, the writer doesn't tell them to bail; instead he tells them to "endure."

In the next chapter, Hebrews 11, the writer describes to the Jewish believers those who made the "Hall of Faith." After listing all of these incredible men and women of faith, notice how the chapter ends:

Through faith [they] conquered kingdoms, enforced justice, obtained promises, stopped the mouths of lions, quenched the power of fire, escaped the edge of the sword, were made strong out of weakness, became mighty in war, put foreign armies to flight. Women received back their dead by resurrection. Some were tortured, refusing to accept release, so that they might rise again to a better life. Others suffered mocking and flogging, and even chains and imprisonment. They were stoned, they were sawn in two, they were killed with the sword. They went about in skins of sheep and goats, destitute, afflicted, mistreated—of whom the world was not worthy—wondering about in deserts and mountains, and in dens and caves of the earth." (Hebrews 11:33–38)

Two things stand out in this passage: (1) the suffering that these men and women of God endured; or to say it another way, these people embraced dis-ease; and (2) their incredible faith. Hebrews 11 shows a clear relationship between suffering and faith. In the process of embracing and experiencing dis-ease, we can exhibit an amazing strength—the two go hand in hand.

"He's Never Failed Me"

As Korie and I are prayerfully considering our role in orphan care, we've asked several of our friends who have adopted to share their experiences with us. We're trying to glean as much wisdom as possible. At one point I was able to contact a guy who recently launched a ministry that encourages people to care for orphans. During a meal with him, I listened to his story.

Our dinner started a little awkwardly. I asked him why he quit his well-paying job in the marketplace, especially given the fact that he had adopted six kids. He shrugged his shoulders and grunted, "God told me to do it." When I asked him how support raising for the ministry was going, he replied, "I don't believe in support raising."

I found this to be both stupid and amazing all at once. How was he taking care of his family? He said he had read a biography on the great nineteenth-century Christian, George Mueller, who was instrumental in the orphan movement in England.

Mueller trusted God so much that he decided to depend on the support for his orphanage without asking anyone for money—or even revealing his needs. He would just trust God completely by prayer, believing that He would provide for him. Not once did God let him down. So inspired by Mueller's life, this man decided to do the same.

Loosening up a bit, he confessed, "It's not easy. I mean there are times when we get down to the wire on things, and we have some real needs. But every time God pulls through in miraculous ways. He's never failed me."

I don't know if I've ever met someone with such amazing faith, with such inner strength. I don't think I would have seen the depth of his faith so clearly if he had not willingly embraced dis-ease as a way of life by quitting his job and entrusting himself fully to the care of God. Needless to say I paid for dinner and then some.

Placing Ourselves at a Disadvantage

Our life of discomfort may not be like that of this adoptive father. And I admit that New Testament passages on suffering and dis-ease are hard to translate into a twenty-first-century context. Our last several presidents have been nothing like the leaders of the Roman Empire who viciously persecuted the Christians. In fact, many of our past presidents have been Christians! So what are we to do with all of the passages in the New Testament on suffering? Are these just tweets?

In *Generous Justice*, Tim Keller helps us to bridge the world of the New Testament, with its themes of suffering, to life in modern day America. He writes, "The strong must disadvantage themselves for the weak, the majority for the minority, or the community frays and the fabric breaks."[2] For Keller, suffering in our context must be voluntarily embraced as Christ-followers choose to disadvantage themselves for the community.

If I could tinker with Dr. Keller's idea of disadvantaging oneself, I would add that it not only has to do with the community, but we disadvantage ourselves for the glory of God. In an age where Christians and non-Christians alike are engaged in social justice, what makes the believer's engagement with the least of these is that we dig wells, build houses, and feed the hungry to the glory of God, not just for the good of the intended recipient.

Disadvantaging oneself for the glory of God and the good of humanity is at the heart of the gospel. We see this in Acts 4:

> Now the full number of those who believed were of one heart and soul, and no one said that any of the things that belonged to him was his own, but they had everything in common. And with great power the apostles were giving their testimony to the resurrection of the Lord Jesus, and great grace was upon them all. There was not a needy person among them, for as many as were owners of lands or houses sold them and brought the proceeds of what was sold and laid it at the apostles' feet, and it was distributed to each as any had need. (32–35)

Acts 4:32–35 shows us the cross-shaped gospel. Right in the heart of the passage we see the apostles proclaiming the resurrection of the Lord Jesus, with "great grace" being present on everyone. This means that people are being connected to God through Jesus Christ. Wrapped around this vertical dimension of the gospel, we see a community of faith that is economically diverse, where those who do not have the financial resources are being cared for by those who do, to the point where no one has a need. The writer of Acts, Luke, notes that those who owned lands and houses sold them and brought the proceeds to the apostles, where the funds were then distributed to help care for the poor in their community. These weren't just people who tithed off of the sale of their land—they gave it all.

Think of the cost involved. Maybe what had been set aside as their children's inheritance is now gone. Maybe this was property where the owners lived, until they came to Jerusalem for the Day of Pentecost (Acts 2), became followers of Jesus Christ, and decided to stay in Jerusalem. So now, not only do they have no home to return to, but they have limited funds to purchase a new home (if any money at all). What these early Christians did was to truly disadvantage themselves.

> So what are we to do with all of the passages in the New Testament on suffering? Are these just tweets?

"Disadvantaging yourself" is exactly how it sounds. It's not merely giving from your abundance, but it's giving to the point of your detriment. It is me allowing myself to experience discomfort so that those around me can have their needs met.

We know Luke is not just talking about people who give generously, because right on the heels of Acts 4:32–35, we are introduced to Ananias and Sapphira. Although this husband and wife agree to sell a piece of property and donate some of the proceeds to the apostles, the story ends with both of them dead. Why? Because they tried to come across as if they were placing themselves at a disadvantage for others. Instead, this couple sought to hold on to comfort by giving only a part of the money from the land they sold (Acts 5:1–2). They lied about giving all the proceeds from the sale to the needy of the church. They refused to disadvantage themselves for others, and this had fatal consequences.

While God may ask us to sell our property and give all of our profits to the poor, I don't think this is the point of the story. If it were, then what do we do with people like Philemon and other wealthy lovers of God who owned property? Instead, I think that what Luke is showing us is that fundamental to the gospel is the need to disadvantage ourselves for others. Ananias and Sapphira's unwillingness to go above and beyond for others reveals a heart that is out of step with the gospel. The heart of the gospel is a Jesus who gave up the comforts of heaven and after three decades on earth, sacrificed Himself by dying on the cross, so that poor debtors like you and me might enjoy the riches of a life connected with Him. Jesus Christ did not simply give from His abundance, but He gave His very life.

A Cross of Comfort?

I sat in a staff meeting at our church once when the discussion centered around what to do with the cross that adorned our stage. We had just moved into a new facility, and because we were renting we had to set up and tear down every week. This was a transition for us, because in our old rented building, we could leave everything as it was, including the cross. Pointing out how heavy the cross would be to move every week, one staff member suggested that we construct a much lighter one in order to ease the burden on the volunteers who needed to move this cross. Without thinking, everyone affirmed the decision. Later on it dawned on me the irony of our conversation, for we wanted to construct a cross that would not burden or cause us the slightest discomfort.

Could this be a fitting parable for so many of us Christians, especially in the West? How many times do we unknowingly embrace comfort at the expense of the cross? Jesus will have none of this. We cannot worship comfort and cling to the old rugged cross at the same time. It is only when we turn our backs on comfort and go the way of the gospel that we will be able to serve others and bring ultimate honor to God.

The Story of Pastor Joe

Some years ago at a Bible conference, another speaker told me his own story of how God had led him to engage the less fortunate. During a trip to Africa, he saw children digging in trash for food and going without water for long periods of time. When he returned to America, he felt nauseated as he looked at his home. Even though he's a pastor of a very large church, making a good salary, and living in a house that's just over two thousand square feet, he was struck with this sense that he needed to do something radical. He knew he needed to experience some dis-ease by voluntarily placing himself at a disadvantage for the glory of God and the good of others. So "Pastor Joe" talked with his family. They agreed with his plan to help others—at a sacrifice to themselves. With his wife's full support, he sold their house and used the proceeds to pay cash for a home just under a thousand square feet. There Joe, his wife, and their four kids now live. Every month they take the money saved from the former mortgage payment and give it to the poor. While there are times when life in such close quarters can become wearisome, nothing can replace the joy that Joe and his family feel by giving their lives away in helping others. This is the gospel.

Practical Ways to Disadvantage Yourself

Maybe as you've been reading you've wondered what are some ways you can embrace discomfort for the glory of God and the good of others.

I know Korie and I have wrestled with this question. Here are three ways to do that. They can become a great source of joy for you and your family and a blessing to others.

First, *invite people to invade your personal space.*

In these tough economic times, the opportunities to show compassion to others by letting them invade our space are great. My wife and I were deeply moved by a TV news report on homeless families in Orlando, where parents had lost their jobs due to the economic downturn. On one stretch of highway, school buses would pull up to hotel parking lots to pick up these displaced children to take them to school.

Later on in the program the news reporter interviewed neighbors who had welcomed a single mother and teenaged son, recently evicted from their home, to live with them until the mother and son could get back on their feet. The neighbors refused to take payment and opened their home, refrigerator, and wallets to this hurting mother and son, allowing them to invade their space. They were willing to disadvantage themselves for the advantage of others. Were these neighbors Christians? It wasn't clear, but they model what those in the family of Christ can and should do as we live out the gospel.

Second, *write an "ouch" check.*

Have you ever experienced a moment when someone has a need and you felt like God wanted you to give toward that need, but to write the check would set you back significantly? It may be time to write what I call an "ouch" check. Don't get me wrong; I'm not talking about writing checks "by faith"; you know, where the money isn't in your account and you hope that by the time the person deposits the check, it miraculously appears. This is just irresponsible. I'm not talking about being a poor steward, but instead going above and beyond in your giving that maybe you have to cut back on your grocery budget for the month.

This is what the early Christians did. Historians tell us that in the early Christian communities when individuals were in such need that they didn't have the resources to eat, sometimes the other Christians, even when they were short on money, would fast and take their daily allotment of food and give to those who were hungry. They didn't just give from their abundance but from their need.

This is what it means to write an "ouch" check. It's not just taking away from the golf or leisure item in your budget, but it's taking away from the essentials for the good of others.

Third, *lay down your rights.*

Harriet Tubman was one of the most courageous people who ever lived. She put her own life on the line when she escaped the slavery down South to live in freedom up North. However, not long after being there she began to think of all her family members and friends who were still in bondage. Sure, she could have argued that she had the right to live in freedom, and if they wanted to have the same freedom, they needed to figure out a way to escape, but she didn't do this. Her love for Jesus, a man who had laid down His rights for her, motivated Harriet Tubman to leave the comforts of life up North, twice a year, to venture down South, putting her own life on the line so that others would be free.

Sure you may have the right to own that second home. Nothing's exactly wrong with that, and you've figured out a way to own multiple homes and give generously to the kingdom. This is your right. But could God be asking you to lay down your rights by selling that home and giving the proceeds to those who can't afford one?

Or maybe as a college student you had planned to work this summer to help pay for tuition in the fall, but an opportunity has come up for you to serve the poor in some urban community. To do this would disadvantage you in a lot of ways, even causing you to sit out a semester—or longer—because you don't have the funds to pay for school. But you sense that God wants you to go on the mission trip anyway, regardless of the personal cost. Sure you have the right to work and pay for school, but maybe God wants you to lay down that right for a short season for His glory and the good of others.

If the emblem of the gospel is the cross—the symbol of dis-ease that became the ultimate sacrifice—then what is the heart of the gospel? It is that we voluntarily embrace dis-ease, putting ourselves at great disadvantage for the glory of God and the good of others.

9 FINISHING WELL

If you want to jubilate over driving the
first spike, go ahead and do it. I don't.
Those mountains over there look too ugly.
We may fail, and if we do, I want to have as
few people know it as we can . . . Anybody
can drive the first spike but there are many
months of labor and unrest between
the first and last spike.[1]

Collis P. Huntington

The building of the transcontinental railroad would revolutionize both travel and business across America. Prior to the laying of two thousand miles of fresh rail tracks from Sacramento, California, to Omaha, Nebraska (and linking with existing tracks originating in New York), a person who wanted to travel from one coast to the other had to choose between two tough routes: a slow wagon trip across country or a sea voyage down the Atlantic Ocean, around the tip of South America, and all the way back up the Pacific. (Believe it or not, it was faster to take to the seas.)[2] All that was about to drastically change with the building of the transcontinental railroad, which began in 1863.

As the men were finally ready to begin the project, they sensed the gravity of the moment. Someone suggested that the constructing of the railroad commence with a major ceremony celebrating the nailing of the first spike. When word reached C. P. Huntington, the project's overseer, he quickly put an end to the party. "We may fail, and if we do, I want to have as few people know it as we can," he wrote in a telegram, adding, "Anybody can drive the first spike but there are many months of labor and unrest between the first and last spike."[3]

Huntington wasn't being a party pooper; he was simply acknowledging that the railroad wasn't going to be built on the adrenaline of excitement. Nothing of lasting value is built and sustained by emotions. There were going to be countless hours filled with sweat and exhaustion. Several men would actually die building the railroad. To finish the project would require there had to be an unrelenting commitment to persevere, to keep pushing when everything in you wanted to quit.

There have been many times in my relationship with Jesus where I have felt the adrenaline rush of the gospel. You may know those moments as well— times when there's an excitement while sharing your faith, praying, reading the Word, putting yourself in discomfort for the sake of others. During such seasons it feels like you've gulped down a huge spiritual energy drink, and the excitement is amazing. But then the season ends, the rush is over, the adrenaline subsides.

> There are many times when I don't *feel* like praying or placing the needs of others above my own.

As a pastor I don't think I'm supposed to say this to you, but it's true: there are many times when I don't *feel* like reading the Bible, praying, or placing the needs of others above my own. Something tells me my story is yours. Now what?

We don't live a cross-shaped gospel on the mountains of adrenaline. Instead, following Jesus takes place among the headaches, difficulties, and pressures of life. How do I live the gospel during the "ugly mountains" of unemployment, or waiting on my wife's biopsy report to come back, or grieving over a struggling child? What we need is perseverance, and a radical commitment to not celebrate over driving the first spike of conversion but at the finish line of "well done."

We have looked at the necessity of dis-ease. Now let's wrestle with the question, How do we practically journey through the discomfort and dis-ease of the cross-shaped gospel? Our guide to the answer is 1 Corinthians 9:24–27. Here Paul describes the necessity of perseverance—and along the way gives us three essential ingredients that, when followed, lead to God saying, "Well done."

The Gospel in 1 Corinthians 9

In the middle of 1 Corinthians 9, Paul invites us into his circle of relationships. We learn that he hangs out with Jews, Gentiles, and religious legalists (to name a few). The picture that comes to mind is Paul eating a kosher meal one day with his Jewish friend, and the next day he's at the local barbecue joint enjoying a slab of ribs with his Gentile buddy. (Of course, being from Memphis, I know those ribs would have been seasoned with dry rub!) Paul's sphere of relationships was eclectic.

But why did Paul go to such lengths to hang out with a diverse group of people, especially people who had to have made him uncomfortable at least initially like the Gentiles? The answer is found in verse 23, where he says that he does all of this "for the sake of the gospel." What inspired Paul's ministry of diversity was the gospel of Jesus Christ. Because Jesus, out of great love, had given His life for Jews and Gentiles, Paul could do no less than to give his life for them, even if it made him uncomfortable. First Corinthians 9 shows us a gospel that connects us to God and connects us to each other regardless of ethnicity.

Right on the heels of talking about the gospel, Paul the apostle offers an image of the Christian who continues to live out the gospel. He writes:

> Do you not know that in a race all the runners run, but only one receives the prize? So run that you may obtain it. Every athlete exercises self-control in all things. They do it to receive a perishable wreath, but we an imperishable. So I do not run aimlessly; I do not box as one beating the air. But I discipline my body and keep it under control, lest after preaching to others I myself should be disqualified. (9:24–27)

The image Paul paints for us in our text is that of a race, and in all likelihood a marathon. It makes sense that Paul would use an athletic metaphor with the Corinthians because every other year they held their version of the Olympics called the Isthmian Games. One of the events at these games was the marathon. If you've ever run one, you know that those who finish the marathon are people who at some point experience difficulty.

Getting through the Runner's Wall

I once had an assistant we'll call Lynne, who ran several marathons throughout the year. I remember asking Lynne about this thing called the runner's wall. She told me that it was that point in the race where in a surreal moment your body turns around, looks at you, and says, "Are you kidding me? Stop! This hurts!" Then Lynne added, "But those who cross the finish line are those who learn to push through the pain." They're people of focus.

Korie and I do a weekly lunch. It's our time to connect with each other. On a recent lunch date we both confided that we're going through one of the most challenging seasons of our lives. It seems like everything is hitting us at once. One of our kids is struggling academically and may need to be held back. We're doing all we can, of course, to help the little guy and to see him through, but we're worried about his confidence as he moves at a little bit of a slower pace. At the same time we're walking through some difficulties with friends and are grieving at least the momentary loss of friendships. We also talked about my leadership challenges, along with other problems that have created a pressure cooker of a season.

On a different occasion I was out of town speaking at an event, and just before I got into bed that night I found myself on my knees weeping before the Lord, begging him for just a quick season of respite from all the problems.

I'm at the point in the marathon of the Christian life where everything within me is screaming, "This hurts! Stop." I've hit the runner's wall.

My grandmother used to say, "We don't live in heaven and board down here." What she was getting at is that Christianity is lived out in the midst of struggling kids, relational difficulties, and leadership challenges. The marathon of the Christian life has its runner's wall. I don't know about you, but when I encounter these seasons, my temptation is to lose all focus on the gospel and the cross and to turn inward. When I do this, things don't get easier. They actually become more difficult.

> A runner breaks through the wall by setting her sights down the road.

When Lynne told me about the runner's wall, I asked her how she would get through it. She said for her the runner's wall normally came at the point in the race where there were still many miles left to run. (Some say it looms at mile eighteen, others mile twenty-one of the twenty-six mile run.) If she was going to get through it, she couldn't think about the finish line, because that was too far off.

"Instead I would pick out an object a hundred or so yards away and focus in on it," Lynne said. "Once I passed that object I found another one and another and another until I got through the really bad pain."

Lynne was able to break through the wall because instead of turning inward and focusing on her problems, as a runner she set her sights down the road. If we're going to be people who finish well and push through the traumatic seasons of life when it feels like our world is caving in, we have to come outside of ourselves by looking "down the road" at the cross.

A Worthy Focal Point

My wife has given birth to three sons, all natural. Most people think that the main reason Korie didn't do the epidural was because of the long needle that goes into the spine, but that's not true. Korie read that going natural was better for the baby, and that was all she needed to hear.

Now, I'll be honest with you: being in the room when your wife is having contractions with no drugs isn't fun for a husband (as if it was for her!). When I compare notes with my buddies who went the epidural route, our experiences are night and day! Our nurses told us that the best way to navigate the intense pain of the contractions is to pick a focus point, concentrate on it, and breathe appropriately. Korie did this. When the contraction came she would squeeze my arm, close her eyes, focus in and breathe; and that's how she was able to make it.

I remember asking her what she was thinking about when she closed her eyes in the midst of those contractions. She told me "the cross." Her thought was if Jesus could endure the suffering of the cross, and if childbirth was not as bad as the cross, then she could get through it. Focusing on the cross pulled her through.

Remember the Hebrews and the difficulty they were going through? Listen to what the writer tells them their focus point needs to be: "Let us also lay aside every weight, and sin which clings so closely, and let us run with endurance the race that is set before us, *looking to Jesus*, the founder and perfecter of our faith, who for the joy that was set before him endured the cross, despising the shame, and is seated at the right hand of the throne of God" (12:1–2, emphasis added). Our focal point, our hope for the future, is Jesus.

What difficulties are weighing you down now? In a down economy your runner's wall could be a season of unemployment or underemployment. Maybe it's the child who has turned their back on Christ and on you. Or your runner's wall could be a medical illness that is cause for concern. If you're like me, your temptation may be to turn inward, to look to yourself and your own network and resources to "figure it out." I want to encourage you, don't turn inward: focus on the cross. Let Christ be your focus point.

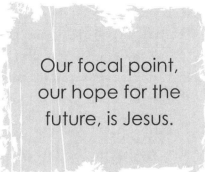

Our focal point, our hope for the future, is Jesus.

The Way through the Wall: Excellence

How can I tell if Christ is my focus point? Paul answers this in our text by showing us three traits that exemplify everyone who hears Jesus say of them, "well done" (see Matthew 25:21). The first is found in 1 Corinthians 9:24, when Paul writes, "Do you not know that in a race all the runners run, but only one receives the prize? So run that you may obtain it." Our passage really hinges on three key words, and the first is found in verse twenty-four when Paul says to "run."

Like all the other books in the New Testament, 1 Corinthians was originally written in Greek. The Greek word for "run" refers to more than just the repetitive movement of a person's feet—it speaks to the heart or the essence of the runner, for it means to give your all. Here Paul helps us to determine if Christ is our focal point, by showing us that those who run the marathon of the Christian life, pushing through the runner's wall and getting to the finish line, are *people marked by excellence*. They give it everything that they have.

When I was a little boy I used to beg my father to sign me up for Little League football at the local park. Our house was right around the corner, so my father would walk me down to Duncan Park where football registration was being held. Signing up for football was pretty elaborate. We'd go from station to station where they would take your weight, measure your height, and finally ask you to pay the registration fee.

Now, my father is a preacher, a very good one, and he doesn't need a stage to preach. He can preach anywhere. Right before he wrote the check to pay the registration fee, he would always preach to me and my brother a two-point sermon that would embarrass us. Dad would remind us that he doesn't make a whole lot of money; in fact, he would say, he was technically not our provider. "God is, and I'm merely a conduit through which God provides." I remember being eight years old and thinking, *What in the world is a conduit*?

> People marked by excellence give it everything that they have.

With a serious look on his face, Dad would assure us that he was more than happy to write the check paying our registration fee, but before he did so we needed to remember that if he paid, we had to stay. In other words, Dad was not trying to hear any excuses that the weather was too hot, the practices too long, or the coach too mean. Crawford Loritts was not going to let us quit. In fact, one year to imprint this point in our minds, he actually walked me home, opened the Loritts family dictionary, took out a pair of scissors, and literally cut out the word "quit." Over the years he loved to remind us that the word "quit" did not even exist in our house!

I've heard many well-meaning Christians suggest that salvation is cheap. Nothing could be further from the truth. Salvation is free, but it most certainly is not cheap. The marathon of the Christian life, like every other marathon, had a registration fee, and ours was paid on a hill called Calvary, when Jesus Christ died the horrible death of crucifixion. The word *excruciating* is rooted in a phrase meaning "out of the cross." Isn't it interesting that a word conveying the most dreadful pain comes from the cross?

> Death by crucifixion was so cruel that the Romans would not allow their citizens to die this way.

Death by crucifixion was seen as one of the cruelest forms of human torture, so cruel that the Romans would not allow their citizens to die this way. This was a slow death, taking on average two to three days. The victims of crucifixion were often seen heaving their bodies upward so that they could breathe, but if you had a nice centurion and he wanted to hurry up and kill you, he would take his club and break your legs so you could no longer push up to get air. It takes my breath away to think that Jesus loved me that much to endure such intense brutality.

Salvation is free, not cheap. I think Jesus is saying the same thing to Christ-followers that my dad used to preach to my brother and me: "Because I've paid, you stay. The word 'quit' should not even be in the Christian's vocabulary. Persevere. Push through the pain like Jesus did and keep running."

You know, there's one other point my dad would make when he would preach his little registration fee homily. He liked to point out that because he was paying this hefty price that he had some expectations. Not only did he want us to resist quitting, but he also wanted us to play hard. Dad didn't like the thought of spending his hard earned money on kids who would just loaf and go through the motions. He wanted us to play to the best of our abilities, to give it our all.

Jesus expects no less from us. His sacrifice on the cross should inspire all-out, Spirit-filled excellence on our part. Sure, we acknowledge that anything I do of eternal value is not me doing it but Christ who does it through me (Philippians 2:12–13); nonetheless, Jesus wants me to surrender and give my all on a moment-by-moment, day-by-day basis.

Is this true of your life, or do you find yourself mindlessly going through the motions? Have you settled for a C or C-minus Christianity, or are you striving for a Hebrews 11, Dean's List kind of faith? If we're going to be people who live a cross-shaped gospel and finish well, we must be people who give it our all, people of excellence.

The Way through the Wall: Endurance

As Paul presses the image of the marathon further, he gives us another necessary trait of anyone who finishes well: "Every athlete exercises self-control in all things. They do it to receive a perishable wreath, but we an imperishable" (9:25). The Greek word for "exercises" is *agonizomai*, from which we get the English words "agony" and "agonize." In a passage where Paul is using the image of the marathon, it makes sense that he would talk about agony, because what he wants us to see is that the marathon of the Christian life, like every other marathon, presupposes pain and problems. It is as if Paul is saying, "Make no bones about it; there will be some *agonizomai*."

Have I lost you at this point? Sadly, many Christians retreat right here. Others have subscribed to what's been called "prosperity theology." That's the idea that if you just give enough money to the Lord, pray, read your Bible, and exercise enough faith, then you will get the brand-new Range Rover with twenty-four-inch rims, or, if you prefer, a Cadillac with run-flat tires. And if you don't receive the vehicle, or you're sick or going through a painful, suffering time, then you must have done

> Following Christ will lead you right to the runner's wall!

something wrong, because God always blesses materially those who obey Him. Those who teach prosperity theology would like for us to believe that anytime a Christ-follower has hit the runner's wall, he or she is outside of God's will, because God would not want any of His children to suffer.

This sounds great, but it's just not true. The people who teach a prosperity gospel must cut out the whole book of Job. Here's a man who suffers greatly, but nothing in the story suggests he did anything wrong. In fact, when God and Satan talk about Job, he's described as a perfect and upright man! These same prosperity teachers have to get rid of the teachings of Jesus. Remember when Christ said that if anyone wanted to come after Him, he had to "take up his cross, and follow [Him]" (Matthew 16:24)?

Even more problematic for the prosperity teachers is the cross of Christ itself. Didn't Jesus experience sickness and suffering on the cross? Yet He did nothing wrong to deserve such abuse. And what do these teachers do with 2 Timothy 3:12, where Paul writes, "Indeed, all who desire to live a godly life in Christ Jesus will be persecuted"? This verse actually says the exact opposite of the prosperity preachers: following Christ won't steer you around the runner's wall; it will lead you right to it!

"Pick Up Something Heavy"

As followers of Jesus Christ, we should expect difficulty, but why? Why would a loving God allow His children to hit the runner's wall, and experience such hardship? I'll never forget the first time I lifted weights. It was the first semester of my sophomore year in a packed gym at Campbell High School. I placed some weights on either side of the bar and sat down at the bench press to do a couple of reps. In the middle of my second set, one of the football coaches marched over to me and demanded that I take the weights that I had placed on the bar and replace them with these huge forty-five-pound plates! Now, I thought I was doing good with my ten-pound weights, and there was no way I was going to lift what amounted to 135 pounds, but you don't say no to your coach, so I decided to make a fool out of myself and trust God for the first time in my life!

The bar came down fast on my chest, and it took everything in me just to break even and keep the bar from going up or down. I'm shaking and sweating. My face is twisting in all kinds of directions, and finally the coach set his clipboard down and began tapping up the bar, whispering in my ear, "Come on, Son; you can do this." This happened two more times, and finally, when he had helped to set the bar back on the rack, he looked me in the eye and said, "Son, fundamental principles to weight lifting: as long as you can lift what you're comfortable with, you'll never get big. But now, if you want to get big, you're just going to have to pick up something heavy."

> Why do we struggle? God is trying to strengthen our faith muscles.

Why does Jesus allow the bar of our lives to get so heavy from time to time? Why do we struggle under the emotional, financial, relational, and health weights at various points? God is trying to get us big, to strengthen our faith muscles. The only way this can happen is to put us into positions where we are forced to trust Him, because we can't possibly lift the weights on our own. He knows that if we want to get big, we have to pick up something heavy.

In our moments of weakness, God assigns to us a spotter called the Holy Spirit. When we think that there's no way we can move another inch, the Holy Spirit begins to lift the bar and whispers in our ear, "You can do all things through Christ who strengthens you; he who is in you is greater than he who is in the world; you are more than conquerors." (See Philippians 4:13; 1 John 4:4; Romans 8:37.)

Whatever it is you're struggling with, or will struggle with, I want to encourage you to not set the bar down. Pray for the strength to endure. Make up your mind right now not to give up but to push through the pain.

The Way through the Wall: Integrity

At the end of our passage Paul writes, "So I do not run aimlessly; I do not box as one beating the air. But I discipline my body and keep it under control, lest after preaching to others I myself should be disqualified" (verses 26–27).

When the Corinthians hosted the Isthmian Games (their version of the Olympics), there would be several different contests. Before each contest a referee would announce the rules to the participants. He would tell them what was permissible and what was not. The word used for the referee announcing the rules to the contestants is the same word translated as "preaching" in verse 27. Paul equates himself to a person who announces the rules, and he says that for anyone who announces the rules and lives a life contrary to the very rules that they announce, they're disqualified. Seeing this, Paul says that he goes to great extremes to make sure he lives with integrity. Integrity is simply the alignment of words with deeds; or to say it another way, integrity means that I do what I say. It's being consistent in word and action.

Paul isn't preaching perfection. Instead, he's pointing to a pattern of life. It could be a parent announcing the rules of the faith to their kids, or a Christian coworker talking about the Scriptures with their coworkers, or a pastor with his congregation. The point that Paul is driving home is that for any Christ-follower who doesn't live what they talk, or practice what they preach, they're disqualified. Now disqualification can't be loss of salvation; how can one lose what they never earned in the first place? And let's remember that the same apostle who writes about disqualification is the one who wrote the most about salvation by grace through faith (Ephesians 2:8–9). So loss of salvation is out of the question. What's in view here, instead, is loss of reward.

I'll never forget my high school graduation. I was so excited to be in my cap and gown and to receive my diploma. As I sat down at the ceremony, I glanced at the program that had a list of all the graduates, and one of the first things that I noticed was that some graduates had a certain set of symbols by their names. One set of symbols meant that Keisha graduated summa cum laude. Another set of symbols meant that Michael graduated magna cum laude. And then there was my name with no set of symbols such as *cum laude*. It just meant that I graduated "Thank You, Laude!" Seriously, as I saw my name with no set of symbols, with no rewards, it caused me to reflect on my tenure in high school. Even though I was graduating and receiving a diploma, I was still sad on this festive occasion. The one thought circling in my head was, *I wish I would have tried a lot harder. I wish I would have burned the midnight oil a little longer.*

Many believers will have a similar experience when they get to heaven. Sure it will be a festive occasion when we see our Savior face-to-face. Just think of the joy that will be ours on that day! But in heaven there will be a rewards ceremony where some Christ-followers will receive crowns. The point of crowns is not to brag, for we'll cast them at the Savior's feet (see Revelation 4:10). For the person who has no crowns, though, I think they'll reflect on their tenure here on earth and wish they had been more diligent in their walk, that they had not given up, that they had pushed through the runner's wall. A loss of integrity means a loss of rewards.

Is your life marked by integrity? Sure, I know all of us fail at certain points to practice what we preach, but as you look at the trajectory of your life, do you see a person who by God's grace is experiencing the alignment of words with deeds? If for some reason you're not walking in integrity, stop right now to ask the Lord's forgiveness and His grace to allow you to finish well.

The cross-shaped gospel produces people who finish well, who push through the runner's wall in excellence, endurance, and integrity. Now what happens when a community of believers marked by the cross-shaped gospel and these three virtues come together? We can expect nothing short of explosive impact on their community. We'll explore this in our next chapter.

10 A CHANGE IS GONNA COME

The greatest need you and I have—the greatest
need of collective humanity—is renovation of
our heart . . . that spiritual place within us from
which outlook, choices, and actions come.[1]

Dallas Willard

In one poignant scene in the film *Malcolm X*, Malcolm is standing outside the local Protestant church in the heart of the city. As the service finally concludes and the worshipers begin pouring out of the doors, Malcolm, a member of the Nation of Islam, greets them by asking what difference their three or so hours in church has made.[2] His question is of course rhetorical, because institutionalized racism, coupled with the systemic problems of life in the inner city, force these church-attending Christ-followers to confess that not much, if anything, has changed. To Malcolm, the verdict has been cast; the church has had very little impact on their community.

Malcolm's assessment of the local church would have definitely been true in my experience. The philosophy of my home church growing up wasn't all that complicated. Members were expected to attend Sunday school at nine-thirty in the morning, followed by worship service at eleven, and then another service that evening. On top of this, the members were expected to attend Wednesday-night Bible study, serve in a ministry, and support the pastor whenever he spoke at a neighboring church within the community. I watched people do this faithfully for years. Looking through the rearview mirror, I can sometimes ask, What difference did all of this church-attending make in my community? Did the schools get better? Was the crime lowered? Did the divorce rate in this same neighborhood decrease? For all of our activity, I'm not sure how many tangible footprints of change we left in our city.

I'm not trying to pick on my home church, because truthfully speaking, the same could be said for most of the churches I've been a part of. I've served in experience-driven churches where people have stood in healing lines and lingered at altar calls. While I don't want to minimize their experience, I do land at the same question of what difference these experiences made in the city or neighborhood around them. I've also worked at event-driven churches where the emphasis was on the next big seminar featuring the world-renowned Bible teacher. I watched as copious notes were being taken by very sincere Christ-followers, but again I have to ask for all the learning, what tangible differences were felt in the community where the church hosting these events was planted?

> Can the church really be an instrument of sustained transformation in the community?

I've also served with churches that were committed to being socially engaged within the community. The hungry were fed. The naked were clothed. Prostitutes were counseled, and the financially indebted were given a fresh start (through generous gifts) and a budget coach. However, even though these churches weren't experience or event driven, I saw the same problem—little long-term transformation through social engagement. It's as if we just hit repeat on a song and kept seeing the same people over and over and over again.

The Church and the Community

My history with the church has caused me to ask, "Can the church really be an instrument of long-term sustained transformation in the community where it's been placed? Or are we just another country club who caters to its members by providing wonderful experiences and events?"

Today I'm still asked the question, "Bryan, why did you come to plant yet another church in Memphis?" This is a good question, especially when you consider that Memphis is the buckle of the Bible Belt. It's Churchville, USA. In fact, someone once said that the average city has one church per thousand people; Memphis has two! But for all her churches, Memphis is also known for her high poverty and crime rates (there's a reality television show that profiles the Memphis Police Department and how it deals with murders in the city), racism (this is the place where Dr. King was killed), and a struggling public school system. Recently, Memphis was profiled on a national television prime-time special on infant mortality because of our high rate of infant deaths.

In Memphis we aspired to be a part of a local body of believers whom God used to proclaim the glorious gospel of Jesus on Sundays and live this gospel throughout the week in such a way that the school system was improved, racism eradicated, and the foster care system completely depleted. In our minds, if the church doesn't imprint its world for the beauty and fame of God, then why bother?

At its core, Memphis is a glaring illustration of a global problem in the body of Christ—that when the cross-shaped gospel is not proclaimed in all of her dimensions, instead of changing the culture, the church actually assists in maintaining and contributing toward the problems of the culture. So I came to Memphis to try and help one church reconnect the two beams of the cross, the horizontal and the vertical. Memphis, and every city in the world, need churches that are committed to a whole gospel that is concerned both with connecting sinful man with a holy God and with one another.

Whenever you and I feel about to fall over the edge into cynicism, let's run to the Acts of the Apostles, the book of the Bible that tells the story of the early church. Here we find both hope and the legacy of true change that is ours, spawned by the first community of believers. If you're like me, you long for something that seeps out of the sermon and four walls on Sundays and into the homes, schools, and shops of your neighborhood. You long to see change.

In Acts 19 the power of the gospel is on display in the city of Ephesus. The monumental influence of the cross-shaped gospel on one of the most popular cities of the world can serve as a guide to reimagining church in our world today. Acts 19 also offers several key principles on how the cross-shaped gospel can bring transformation in our individual lives as well as our churches.

The Church and the World

According to Acts 19:1, "Paul passed through the inland country and came to Ephesus." Ephesus was the New York City of its day, with a large population and a strategic port at the Aegean Sea. Its main attraction was the temple of Artemis, one of the seven wonders of the ancient world. Artemis was the goddess of fertility. If a couple had a problem conceiving, the man took a trip to Ephesus and paid homage to Artemis in the hopes that they would become fertile.

> Scripture points to a church that is actively engaged in the world around it.

Ephesus, like New York, was seen as a progressive city, one of the few places where women had a voice. Ephesus was founded by a tribe of female warriors, and from this beginning the feminist spirit prospered in Ephesus.[3] The Bible gives us a hint of the unprecedented place that women had in Ephesus, because some of Paul's strongest instructions on the role of women in the church were written to Timothy, pastor of the church at Ephesus (1 Timothy 2:8–15).

Paul knew that establishing a gospel beachhead in a place like Ephesus would be huge for advancing the kingdom of God. So he made his way to the city to proclaim the gospel and form a community of believers. His goal was to transform the city.

Sometimes I find myself forgetting basic truths, truths like the church isn't a country club that exists to cater to its members, but is called to influence its city and country. Take some moments to remind yourself of what the Bible says that we as Christ-followers and the church should be about:

Then he said to his disciples, "The harvest is plentiful, but the laborers are few; therefore pray earnestly to the Lord of the harvest to send out laborers into his harvest." (Matthew 9:37–38)

"What I tell you in the dark, say in the light, and what you hear whispered, proclaim on the housetops. And do not fear those who kill the body but cannot kill the soul. Rather fear him who can destroy both soul and body in hell." (Matthew 10:27–28)

"All authority in heaven and on earth has been given to me. Go therefore and make disciples of all nations, baptizing them in the name of the Father and of the Son and of the Holy Spirit, teaching them to observe all that I have commanded you. And behold, I am with you always, to the end of the age." (Matthew 28:18–20)

How then will they call on him in whom they have not believed? And how are they to believe in him of whom they have never heard? And how are they to hear without someone preaching? And how are they to preach unless they are sent? As it is written, "How beautiful are the feet of those who preach the good news!'" (Romans 10:14–15)

All these passages of Scripture point to a church that is actively engaged in the world around it. These texts do not paint the picture of a church that's turned inward having settled for a calendar full of events or experiences. Is there a place for events? Absolutely. Paul tells the Ephesians that the church exists to equip people (Ephesians 4:11–12). A part of what it means to equip is that we need to teach our people, arming them with the appropriate tools to be effective ambassadors for Christ. But we must never forget that our equipping must be done with the goal of engaging our communities and world for the glory of God.

Paul's Christ-Centered Preaching

Paul had the same aspirations when he walked into Ephesus. Paul comes to Ephesus with one goal in mind—to transform the city for the glory of God. How will he do this? Through the gospel of Jesus Christ, and specifically what we've been calling the cross-shaped gospel. We see this cross-shaped gospel in Acts 19:8, which says of Paul: "He entered the synagogue and for three months spoke boldly, reasoning and persuading them about the kingdom of God." Later on we would find Paul on Gentile turf, "reasoning daily in the hall of Tyrannus. This continued for two years, so that all the residents of Asia heard the word of the Lord, both Jews and Greeks" (9b–10).

What did Paul's "reasoning" center around? The gospel. Whether with the Jews in the synagogue, or the Greeks in the hall of Tyrannus, Paul proclaimed to them the person of Jesus Christ, showing them their sins and how they could have a relationship with God through His Son. His preaching did not center around feel good themes, or motivational messages that diluted or altogether left out the person and work of Christ. Instead his preaching was what we would call Christocentric—Christ centered!

This is the heartbeat and essence of the gospel. It would be Paul's Christ-centered preaching that would lay the groundwork for all-encompassing transformation of Ephesus.

Every Sunday at our church, when I take the text, my aim is to "make a beeline for the cross" as Charles Spurgeon put it. No matter the Scripture I'm preaching on, I want to show people the gospel by presenting Christ crucified, and the only means of forgiveness of sins. This gospel-centered preaching has yielded rich fruit in our body. It's a common sight to see people standing in line to receive Communion after the message (we take Communion every week) with tears trickling down their cheeks. Often I will receive e-mails from these individuals in which they tell me how the gospel is changing them.

One young man ventured into our church and heard the gospel for the first time. He was a self-described fornicator, addicted to pornography, women, and status. The only reason he came to our church is because a woman he was interested in attended, and he figured this would be a great way to seduce her. Yet after months of hearing the gospel, his heart began to change, until he finally yielded his life to Christ and renounced his former way of life. He's led people to faith in Jesus and is leading a Bible study that has been a source of great inspiration to many. The gospel has done nothing less than to transform him.

We don't need a church in order to proclaim man's need for a Savior. We can do this anywhere. Just recently my wife and I were in London, in a taxicab on our way to the airport to return home. As I was talking to the cab driver, it became clear that he was not a follower of Jesus Christ and I felt the Spirit nudging me to share with him the good news of the empty tomb. Even though I've studied Greek and Hebrew and serve as a pastor, I still get nervous when it comes to sharing the gospel one-on-one with people. I don't want to be rejected or categorized as some condemning, legalistic "fundamentalist." But my love for Jesus and the thought of someone spending an eternity in hell pushes me past my selfish desires of acceptance.

So I cleared my throat and shared with him the good news of Jesus Christ. No, he didn't pray with me to accept Christ, but a seed was planted. Like Paul, we need to boldly proclaim man's desperate need for a holy God and selfless Savior.

"Pure and Undefiled"

Paul's ministry in Ephesus begins with him preaching the vertical dimensions of the gospel—man's total need of a Savior. Yet there's more: "And God was doing extraordinary miracles by the hands of Paul, so that even handkerchiefs or aprons that had touched his skin were carried away to the sick, and their diseases left them and the evil spirits came out of them" (Acts 19:11–12). The sick and demon-oppressed in Ephesus were finding healing and relief. People were tangibly bettered through the ministry of Paul. Once again we see the cross-shaped gospel at work, as people's souls are being made new along with their bodies. The cross-shaped gospel laid the foundation for the transformation of Ephesus.

Paul's ministry was not confined inside the walls of the local synagogue or the hall of Tyrannus. It spilled out in ways that blessed the people of Ephesus spiritually and physically. This is the recipe for transformation—the cross-shaped gospel where souls and bodies are being cared for and ministered to.

Just as the two beams of the cross that crucified Jesus were tied to one another, so are the vertical and horizontal "beams" of the gospel. When the gospel of Jesus Christ regenerates our hearts, it shows through in churches and lives that care for the needs of the hurting around them. In fact, to separate the two is to create a false gospel. James the brother of Jesus writes, "Religion that is pure and undefiled before God, the Father, is this: to visit orphans and widows in their affliction, and to keep oneself unstained by the world" (1:27). Later on James would write:

> What good is it, my brothers, if someone says he has faith but does
> not have works? Can that faith save him? If a brother or sister is
> poorly clothed and lacking in daily food, and one of you says to
> Them, "Go in peace, be warmed and filled," without giving them
> the things needed for the body, what good is that? So also faith by
> itself, if it does not have works, is dead (2:14–17).

James, along with the whole of the Scriptures, affirms that there is no
such thing as a gospel that does not link a regenerated heart with generous, benevolent acts toward those in need.

Pastor Jeff (not his real name) is a friend of mine who once received
a strange request. His leadership team *demanded* that he take a vacation.
You would think no one would need to be told to take a vacation, but Pastor Jeff hadn't taken one in years. The reason he hadn't was because whenever he would get extra money, he felt compelled to give it to the poor. Sure
there's a bit of unhealthiness in my friend not taking his breaks, yet his actions reveal a heart that is so grateful to God that he longs to give, even at
the expense of himself and his family.

You don't have to be a pastor to practice generosity to those in need.
All of us are called to live out the gospel in many ways and various times
to show that the gospel is both attractive and life changing.

Gospel Footprints

In Ephesus, people were obsessed with the supernatural. It was just a
part of their culture. I think this is why Paul, in writing to the church in
Ephesians 6, spends more time talking about spiritual warfare than he did
with any other church, because he knew that there was a serious demonic
stronghold in the city.

We get a clear picture of how deep the people of Ephesus dabbled in the occult in the middle of Acts 19 where Paul, after having labored to proclaim and live the gospel, saw the fruits of the Spirit's work through him. The text tells us that these brand-new Christ-followers came "confessing and divulging their practices. And a number of those who had practiced magic arts brought their books together and burned them in the sight of all. And they counted the value of them and found it came to fifty thousand pieces of silver. So the word of the Lord continued to increase and prevail mightily" (18–20).

One scholar suggests that the value of the books that they burned equals about six million dollars in today's currency![4] I mean this is unthinkable on two levels: first, that the people of Ephesus were so devoted to the occult to spend such money; and second, the power of the gospel to bring about such a sweeping repentance. The city of Ephesus was transformed.

> Paul's preaching— and living—the gospel shook the foundations of Ephesus.

Right on the heels of their public renunciation of their former life and embracing this gospel, there arose a complaint by a silversmith named Demetrius. In short, he's upset because the transformation of Ephesus was having a widespread economic impact on the city and even the region. The words of Demetrius, a local idol maker, testify to the transformation Ephesus was experiencing:

And you see and hear that not only in Ephesus but in almost all of Asia this Paul has persuaded and turned away a great many people, saying that gods made with hands are not gods. And there is danger not only that this trade of ours may come into disrepute but also that the temple of the great goddess Artemis may be counted as nothing, and that she may even be deposed from her magnificence, she whom all Asia and the world worship. (26–27)

Do you see what this non-Christ-follower is saying? The gospel is not only having a significant economic impact but is threatening one of the seven wonders of the ancient world, the very soul of Ephesus—Artemis! Paul's preaching—and living—the gospel shook the economic, cultural, and religious foundations of Ephesus.

I want this for my neighborhood. I want this for your workplace, athletic league, schools, and community. I want to so preach and live Jesus Christ that I leave huge gospel footprints wherever I go, being an agent of change.

The question is, Do we believe this? Do we believe that the same gospel Paul preached and practiced can yield the same results through our lives in the various spheres that we traffic in? I mean do we really believe this?

Believe in a Big and Powerful God

Paul traveled to Ephesus because he believed that the gospel is big and powerful enough to transform this global city. Why else would Paul even bother to come, unless he was fully convinced? If we're going to experience gospel transformation through our lives, we must begin with belief in a powerful gospel, with fully convinced hearts that say, "Yes, God can use us as His instruments for extreme gospel makeovers that rattle the economic, religious, cultural, and political spheres of our society."

This is why I came to Memphis, because I was sure that God was calling me to be a part of something that was beyond Sunday mornings; God wanted nothing less than for me to be a vessel He wields to change Memphis.

When our family landed in Memphis, one of the first things I did was to contact different church leaders in the city to ask them for their wisdom. Over a meal I would share with them my desire to plant a gospel-centered, disciple-making, multiethnic church. Without fail, when it came to the multiethnic part, each leader said that while my aspirations were noble, this would never happen in Memphis because the racism was too entrenched. Do you see what they're saying? These men were telling me that the gospel was not powerful enough to change our city. At some point they had stopped believing; they had abandoned their faith in the changing power of the gospel, and the legacy of that has been a city that is still wallowing in the sins of her past.

There are many "Christians" who are not believers. There are plenty of people who claim to follow Jesus Christ but don't really believe that God can use them on the battlefields of their neighborhoods and fraternity houses to provoke change. So we settle for our comfortable and normal lives and miss out on the impossible movements of God. We'll never see our own Ephesus changed until we believe.

Get Out of the Boat!

Change doesn't happen on a whiteboard in some great strategic planning session. Nor is change the product of faith or good intentions. Transformation only happens when there is intentional engagement with the very people you want to see changed. Paul models this beautifully in Acts 19. I'm sure he spent a lot of time praying for the people of Ephesus, but at some point it was time to get off of his knees. So Paul gets up and goes to the synagogue and proclaims the gospel. Paul had a sincere heart for the Gentiles and prayed for them as well. When he whispered "amen," ending his prayer time, he taught in the hall of Tyrannus. After he finished teaching, Paul didn't disengage from the people, but he labored right in their midst. We know this because the people of Ephesus were able to take his handkerchiefs or aprons he had touched and use them for healing. How did change happen in a global city like Ephesus? Paul intentionally engaged the people, the very ones he longed to see transformed.

I use prayer cards to help me focus in on specific requests for individuals I'm praying for. Some time ago I drew up a prayer card for a friend of mine I was feeling some relational distance with. Several times a week I would take this prayer card out and pray for this person and our relationship, asking God to move in very precise ways to bring warmth back to our friendship. A few months later I was praying through this request again, frustrated why nothing had happened, and in that moment it was as if God said, "Of course nothing has happened; you haven't done anything. Don't you think you should call him, take him out to lunch maybe? Just do something!" I had to laugh at this earth-shattering "revelation"! I was asking God to move, yet I was unwilling to move myself! In this moment the words of James came to mind, "faith apart from works is dead" (James 2:26).

Be careful about praying for change, because in my experience God often has a way of using us as a means to answer our own prayers. Sometimes the reason why we're not seeing the kind of transformation we long for in our neighborhoods, workplaces, or campuses is because we're unwilling to be the instrument He uses to spark the change. As pastor and author John Ortberg has famously quipped, "If you want to walk on water, you've got to get out of the boat." Big-time movements of God normally begin with small, intentional steps by His people.

Allen, a dedicated Christian, had been extremely successful in the financial industry, where he made a great deal of money. But his heart ached for one impoverished community in Memphis, and he realized that it wasn't enough for him to pray and give some of his money to help make things better in the hood. He sensed that God was asking him to be personally engaged with the very people he wanted to see the gospel change. So Allen quit his job and joined the leadership of a nonprofit organization that helped to build and renovate homes in this community.

Now, several years later, this same community has caught a second wind and is making a sincere turnaround. Volunteers continue to renovate housing by doing such tasks as replacing shingle roofs and rotten floors, doing plumbing and drywall repairs, and painting or siding old homes.

When homeowners can't afford such needed repairs, Christian volunteers do all of this as a means to proclaim the gospel of Jesus Christ in word and deed. This happened in large part because my friend got out of the boat and into the action.

Korie and I have another friend who was heartbroken over the pandemic of fatherlessness in the African-American community. James (not his real name) and his wife began to pray for revival in African-American homes, that strong godly men would be raised up. This couple attended a "Weekend to Remember" Family Life marriage conference and God spoke to them: they needed to figure out a way to bring what they just experienced at this conference back to the black community. Their own children were "out of the nest" and doing well, but James wanted to reverse the tide of fathers who were leaving their children and wives. Through hard work and partnerships with other African-American leaders, dozens of conferences were hosted over the next ten or so years, where thousands of African-American marriages were strengthened through the leadership of this couple. Transformation began to happen when they yielded themselves as the tools God could use to spark a movement.

What about you? Where does your heart ache to see God move? Where's your Ephesus, that place that you so long to see transformed but seems to be at the same time in the realm of the impossible? Remember, Ephesus was only changed when Paul, armed with the gospel and filled with the Spirit, walked intentionally into the city. What intentional steps do you need to take to unleash the cross-shaped gospel in your Ephesus?

Care Deeply about People

One chapter later in Acts 20, we see Paul leaving the Ephesians. After three years with them, he had grown close to them. His intimate care and concern for them is documented by Luke: "And when he had said these things, he knelt down and prayed with them all. And there was much weeping on the part of all; they embraced Paul and kissed him, being sorrowful most of all because of the word he had spoken, that they would not see his face again. And they accompanied him to the ship" (20:36–38).

Luke paints a very emotional scene. There's praying and weeping and embracing. Earlier, reflecting on his three years of ministry with them, Paul said that he taught them "with tears" (20:31). The Ephesians weren't some project to Paul, but they were people whom he loved and cared for deeply, even to the point of tears.

A few years ago I was preaching on compassion to a group of people involved in homeless ministry. My opening remarks expressed the obvious: "Why in the world would a guy talk about compassion to people who feel called to give their lives away to the homeless?" I went on to explain that one of the great ironies of ministry is that we can stop caring for the very ones we've been called to minister to. We can, in the words of John Piper, become professionals (Piper's book is entitled *Brothers, We Are Not Professionals*). People can become projects, mere numbers to put on our prayer letters that we send out several times a year in the hopes of raising more support to meet our personal or operating budgets. I know of far too many leaders who preach and minister without ever shedding a tear for their people. This shouldn't be.

> I know of far too many leaders who preach and minister without ever shedding a tear for their people.

Pedro's Passion

If you had lived in Cartagena, Columbia, in the early part of the seventeenth century, you would have been astounded by a man known as Pedro Claver. The title this Colombian priest gave to himself was highly unusual considering the times. He called himself Pedro, the servant of black slaves. When a slave ship would come to town, Pedro would be the first to greet the disembarking slaves. As you can imagine, many of these slaves were severely malnourished, sick, and lacked adequate clothing. Pedro would immediately greet them with baskets of food and clothes. He would even carry the sick slaves to the local hospital and make sure that their needs were properly taken care of. Many of these slaves had even contracted leprosy.

Instead of retreating, Pedro chose to start his own leprosarium in order to meet their needs. He would even endanger his own life by embracing and hugging these lepers.

Yet the ministry of Pedro Claver was not just a social ministry that assisted the physical needs of the least of these. He also addressed their most significant need—a Savior. Not long after the slaves would arrive, Pedro would gather them together in a circle and would preach the gospel of Jesus Christ to them, leading many of them to the faith. Once they were saved he felt strongly that they needed to be instructed in the doctrines of the faith, so he labored tirelessly to teach them. For example, when teaching them the doctrine of the Trinity, he would pull out a handkerchief, fold it so that the three corners could clearly be seen, and show them that while the cloth had three corners, it was still one piece of cloth.

Pedro Claver preached a whole gospel—addressing both the physical and spiritual needs of these people. And yet all of his preaching, teaching, feeding, clothing, and caring came from one fundamental virtue—his great compassion for them. Any observer would have to confess that these slaves were not some project to Pedro. He loved them. He had great compassion for them, and it was out of this compassion that his ministry flowed, transforming their lives.[5]

Do our neighbors know that we love them? What about the immoral ones on our jobs or in our dormitories; do they feel compassion from us? The people we long to see transformed must know that we care deeply for them. The people of Ephesus knew Paul loved them, and that opened their hearts to the truth of the gospel that he shared with them, setting the stage for citywide transformation. May the same be true of us.

NOTES

Introduction: From the Shadow of the Cross

1. John Stott, *The Cross of Christ* (Downers Grove, Ill.: InterVarsity, 1986), 17. Hunt painted "The Shadow of Death" while in the Holy Land from 1870–73.
2. So described by George Bennard in verse 1 of his classic hymn, "The Old Rugged Cross."

1. The Gospel in Two-Part Harmony

1. As quoted in John Stott, *The Cross of Christ* (Downers Grove, Ill.: InterVarsity, 2006), 21.
2. Story taken from a Tony Campolo message at the Christian Leadership Conference, February 18, 2011, The Boulders, Scottsdale, Arizona; sponsored by the Young Presidents Organization.
3. Lewis Drummond, *Charles Spurgeon: Prince of Preachers* (Grand Rapids: Kregel, 1992), 397.
4. Arnold Dallimore, *George Whitefield*, vol. 2 (Carlisle, Penn: Banner of Truth: 1980), 591, and vol.1 (Carlisle, Penn: Banner of Truth: 1970), 391.
5. Ibid, vol. 2, 368.
6. Ibid.
7. Rob Moll, "Billy Graham, the Unifier," posting at Christianity Today Library.com; http://www.ctlibrary.com/newsletter/newsletterarchives/2004-07-09.html.
8. "Billy Graham: An Appreciation," *Baptist History and Heritage*, June 22, 2006; as cited in Wikipedia, "Billy Graham"; http://en.wikipedia.org/wiki/Billy_Graham.

2. Reaching Out by First Reaching Up

1. J. Gresham Machen, *Christianity and Liberalism* (Grand Rapids: Eerdmans, 1923), 128.
2. George Marsden, *Understanding Fundamentalism and Evangelicalism* (Grand Rapids: Eerdmanns, 1991), 101.
3. I personally hold to progressive dispensationalism, because it does believe that while aspects of the kingdom are yet future, there is at the same time a very present sense of the kingdom that demands the church's engagement with society.

4. Harvey Cox, *The Future of Faith* (New York: HarperOne, 2009), 19.

3. Donkeys and Elephants

1. Jason J. Stellman, *Dual Citizens* (Lake Mary, Fla.: Reformation Trust, 2009), xxv.

4. The Gospel and O. J. Simpson

1. Cornel West, *Hope on a Tightrope* (Carlsbad, Calif.: Hay House, 2008), 59.

2. In 1992, police officers were accused of excessive force during the arrest of black motorist Rodney King. A police video used in court showed a repeated beating of the suspect. Three of the police officers were found innocent, and angry protesters touched off the Los Angeles riots. Many felt the officers were guilty, and even President George H. W. Bush questioned the verdict. See "Rodney King," *Wikipedia*, http://en.wikipedia.org/wiki/Rodney_King.

3. Tony Evans, *Tony Evans' Book of Illustrations* (Chicago: Moody, 2009), 202.

5. The Other Side of the Tracks

1. Tim Keller, *Generous Justice* (New York: Dutton, 2010), 180.

2. Randy Alcorn, *Money, Possessions and Eternity* (Carol Stream, Ill.: Tyndale, 2003), 3.

3. Ibid.

6. The Gospel and the Glory of God

1. Viktor E. Frankl, *Man's Search for Meaning* 3d ed. (New York: Simon & Schuster, 1984), 9. He actually quotes Nietzsche, who said it originally.

2. Philip Yancey, *Rumors of Another World* (Grand Rapids: Zondervan, 2003), 223–24.

7. Declaring the Whole Truth

1. Os Guinness, *Prophetic Untimeliness* (Grand Rapids: Baker, 2005), 9.

2. Stephen Ambrose, *Nothing Like It in the World* (New York : Simon & Schuster, 2001), 250.

8. Getting Comfortable with a Life of Dis-ease

1. Quoted in Malcolm Gladwell, *What the Dog Saw* (New York: Little. Brown, 2009), n.p., as cited in "Book Review: What the Dog Saw," at www.robchristeson.com/book-review.

2. Tim Keller, *Generous Justice* (New York: Dutton, 2010), 180.

9. Finishing Well

1. As quoted in Stephen Ambrose, *Nothing Like It in the World: The Men Who Built the Transcontinental Railroad* (New York: Simon and Schuster, 2001), 117.

2. The wagon ride would take up to 190 days. For this and other information on the building of the historic railroad, see ""What Are the Facts about the Transcontinental Railoroad?" at www.wiki.answers.com/Q/What_are_facts_about_ the_trans_continental_railroad; and in Ambrose, *Nothing Like It in the World*.

3. As quoted in Ambrose, *Nothing Like It*, 117.

10. A Change Is Gonna Come

1. Dallas Willard, *Renovation of the Heart* (Colorado Springs: NavPress, 2002), 14.

2. Greeting worshipers at Protestant churches after Sunday services was a common tactic of the Nation of Islam. During the 1950s and 1960s, Nation of Islam members intentionally recruited from the black church. See Malcolm X and Alex Haley, *The Autobiography of Malcolm X.*

3. All background on the city taken from Dr. Ray Vander Laan, leader of Holy Land tours, lecture notes from "In the Footsteps of the Disciples," a trip to Ephesus I took with him in May of 2007.

4. *ESV Study Bible* (Wheaton: Crossway Bibles, 2007), note on Acts 19:19.

5. Justo Gonzalez, *The Story of Christianity*, vol. 1 (New York: HarperOne, 2010), 392–94.

ACKNOWLEDGMENTS

This book is the result of years of experiences and being shaped by countless individuals, so there's no way I could possibly thank everyone who should be acknowledged for this project. However, there are several people I must mention, without which this book would not be possible.

My bride, Korie, played an integral part, reading the chapters as I wrote them and providing gracious feedback. Her influence stretches past the mere writing of pages, though. Korie's gift of mercy has pushed our family to live the cross-shaped gospel specifically in the realm of justice and compassion.

Greg Thornton, vice president of publishing with Moody, has been a longtime friend of our family and was responsible for getting this project started. Jim Vincent and Dave DeWit were extremely valuable in the editing process, providing me both with encouragement and loving pushback where needed.

I am blessed to have the best assistant on the planet in Danielle Ridley, who worked hard to guard my calendar, providing wonderful space for me to get away and write.

Much of what you will read in this book is the fruit of my service to Fellowship Memphis as the lead pastor. I feel extremely blessed to work with such a great church and to be a small part of what God is doing in our city. Jason Holbrook, Hamp Holcomb, John Bryson, Ben Parkinson,

Randy Odom, Hasaan Saleem, Jay Harvill, and Roy "Soup" Campbell make up our elder team at Fellowship Memphis. I am so thankful that these men excitedly share me with the broader body of Christ, giving me time to write and preach outside the church.

Last but certainly not least, I must stop and thank my parents, Dr. Crawford and Karen Loritts. I am blessed to have two parents who have been married over forty years, who not only love each other deeply, but love God authentically. Their influence in my life is immeasurable and anything I become in this life is ultimately because of the sovereign grace of God working through my parents who helped to cultivate a heart that loves Jesus. I only hope that I can continue this legacy with my three boys, Quentin, Myles, and Jaden.